KEEPING
HOUSE

JB JOSSEY-BASS

KEEPING HOUSE

The Litany of Everyday Life

Margaret Kim Peterson

BICENTENNIAL
1807
WILEY
2007
BICENTENNIAL

John Wiley & Sons

Published by Jossey-Bass
A Wiley Imprint
989 Market Street, San Francisco, CA 94103-1741   www.josseybass.com

Readers should be aware that Internet Web sites offered as citations and/or sources for
further information may have changed or disappeared between the time this was written
and when it is read.

Jossey-Bass books and products are available through most bookstores. To contact Jossey-Bass
directly call our Customer Care Department within the U.S. at 800-956-7739, outside the
U.S. at 317-572-3986, or fax 317-572-4002.

Jossey-Bass also publishes its books in a variety of electronic formats. Some content that
appears in print may not be available in electronic books.

Library of Congress Cataloging-in-Publication Data
Peterson, Margaret Kim, Date.
Keeping house : the litany of everyday life / Margaret Kim Peterson. —
1st ed.
        p. cm.
   Includes bibliographical references.
   ISBN-13: 978-0-7879-7691-0
   ISBN-10: 0-7879-7691-1
   1. Home—Religious aspects—Christianity. 2. Housekeeping. I. Title.
   BR115.H56P48 2007
   248.4—dc22   2006103360

Printed in the United States of America
FIRST EDITION
HB Printing   10 9 8 7 6 5 4 3 2 1

CONTENTS

In memory of
Lily Ann Mutter,
May 14, 1998–August 14, 1998

ACKNOWLEDGMENTS

As I thought about writing this book and then as I actually undertook writing it, I talked about the project with many of my colleagues, acquaintances, and friends. Their responses fell into four categories. The men, with few exceptions, said either "Hmmm" or "My wife should read that book." The women, with few exceptions, said either "You've got to be kidding!" or "I want to read that book!" I hope that the book I have written will be of interest to members of all those groups: the men who were bored, the men who thought their wives might like it, the women who were horrified, and the women who were intrigued! In any event, thanks are due to all those conversation partners. This is not a book that could have been written in the isolation of a study or library, and I appreciate the willingness of so many friends to talk about the project with me.

Additional support for this book was provided by stipends from the Louisville Institute and the Valparaiso Project on the Education and Formation of People in Faith and by my home congregation, First Presbyterian Church of Norristown, Pennsylvania, which provided me with an office in which I worked in peaceful quiet during one of my son's more rambunctious summers. My most heartfelt thanks go, of course, to my husband, Dwight, who makes a sublime risotto, and to my son, Mark, whose enthusiasm for washing dishes, floors, and cars knows no bounds.

PREFACE

Most books have multiple beginnings. Among the beginnings of this book were conversations I had a few years ago with a couple of women friends. Each was somewhere in midlife, busy at church and at home and at work. And each was ready for a change, although it wasn't entirely clear what kind of change was possible or desirable. In talking with each of these friends, I raised the question what she might do if all options were open and money was no object. And in each case my friend burst into tears and said, "I would make a home for my family."

It turned out that each friend's family was dependent on her continued full-time employment outside the home for their health insurance. As a result, each of these women felt locked into a life in which the work of making a home had to be fit in around the edges of unyieldingly long hours laboring at her profession. And too much of the time it seemed as if the work of making a home could not be fit in, that home and family lurched along, barely nurtured, barely sustained, required always to make do with much less than would be comfortable or beautiful or desirable.

Neither of my friends had great housekeeping ambitions. Neither desired a home that was grandiose or spotless.

They just wanted curtains at the windows and meals on the table, clothes neatly hung and folded rather than lying in neglected heaps, and enough predictability and order for it to be easy and pleasurable to invite others in for a visit or a meal. And each wanted to do this work herself. It wasn't that either of them aspired to do nothing but keep house or that either wanted to keep house all by herself, with no contribution from spouse or children or hired help. It seemed rather to be that each of these women sensed, in some place deep in her soul, that the disciplines involved in feeding and clothing and sheltering others, beginning with the members of their own households, were profoundly worthwhile, and it grieved them that they could devote so little of themselves to so life-giving a work.

I came away from those conversations wondering what the church had to say to my friends. The resources of the Christian tradition—scripture, theology, pastoral, and spiritual wisdom—speak to so many of the challenges of life in thought-provoking and encouraging ways. What might those resources have to offer someone striving to find the time and the energy to keep house in trying circumstances?

Another of the beginnings of this book came toward the beginning of my own professional life. I had started my first official teaching job, which, as it happened, was a half-time position. I was happy for it to be so, since my husband's job provided enough additional money to make ends meet (plus health insurance!), and I could then have enough time to settle and care for us in the new city to which we had moved. But we had no children, and when new acquaintances discovered that I worked "only" half time, they would ask, "So what do you do with the rest of your time?" "I keep house," I would say.

That was always the end of the conversation. I had the uncomfortable sense that virtually any other answer would have been more acceptable. People would have been happy to hear that I was an artist or a writer, that I was developing a small business, that I was practicing the piano or taking flying lessons. But keeping house? I might as well have said, "I'm wasting my time."

It didn't seem like a waste of time to me. I was busy every day with marketing, cooking, laundry, making beds, tidying up, the occasional halfhearted swipe at real dirt (cleaning has never been my strong suit). And the result was that my husband and I had fresh clothes to put on in the morning and a good meal to sit down to at night and the freedom and flexibility to have friends in for dinner or to carry a casserole to a family with illness or a new baby in the house. That seemed pretty worthwhile to me.

As I thought about it, though, I realized that I was virtually the only person I knew who was my age or younger and who neither worked full time nor had small children at home. It didn't seem to matter how much money people had or where their health insurance came from; if they did not have small children (and in many cases even if they did), they worked full time and fit their housekeeping in around the edges or hoped someone else would do it.

I didn't begrudge any of my friends their jobs; they were, many of them, doing interesting and worthwhile work and contributing in a wide variety of ways both to their families and to the broader community. But why was it that not a single other one of them had made the choice I had, to keep house with more than leftover bits of time? Was keeping house really a waste of time, at best a hobby to be indulged in by people who like that sort of thing and at worst an unpleasant set of necessary chores? Or were there broader cultural and theological factors that made housekeeping seem like all of these things when in fact it was, as I had found it, a discipline as interesting and worthwhile as many other kinds of work?

A third beginning of this book (although the earliest in time of the stories I have told here) came just before the beginning of that first teaching job. I had finished my graduate program in the spring and was due to move house toward the end of the summer. Although my husband and I hardly had two nickels to rub together, we agreed that I would not seek paid employment for those few months and would instead devote my time to getting us packed and moved. I would, in other words, be "just a housewife."

Around that time my friend Donna gave birth to her second child. Lily turned out to be severely affected by Down syndrome. She spent the three months of her brief life in a pediatric intensive-care nursery, and for those three months Donna practically lived at the hospital with her. I sat and visited with them for a couple of hours two or three days a week, sharing with them in that searing experience of love and loss. Lily died just a week after we moved; we had been gone from church only one Sunday before we were back for her funeral.

All that fall I mourned for Lily, and I wondered how it was that her life and mine and Donna's had touched so briefly and so deeply. I had, in fact, hardly known Donna before that summer. Why was it that I had spent so much time at the hospital with her and Lily? I realized eventually that to a large degree, I did it because I could do it. Donna and her family were surrounded by a large and supportive church community, but I was virtually the only person who was not busy all day with either work or child care. I was just a housewife.

Those months with Donna and Lily reminded me that time deliberately set aside for keeping house is never just about "making a home for my family." Of course housework is about making a home, but a Christian home, properly understood, is never just for one's own family. A Christian

home overflows its boundaries; it is an outpost of the kingdom of God, where the hungry are fed and the naked are
clothed and there is room enough for everyone.

Keeping house can be a very mundane activity. It is certainly repetitive, and the kinds of work that it involves are
varied enough that few people enjoy all of them equally. But
at the very same time, housekeeping is about practicing
sacred disciplines and creating sacred space, for the sake of
Christ as we encounter him in our fellow household members and in neighbors, strangers, and guests. Lily, in her fleet-
ing appearance among us, was in some sense all of these. This
book is dedicated to her.

KEEPING HOUSE

1

What's Christian About Housework?

I have always enjoyed keeping house. From my earliest childhood I wanted to cook, so my mother taught me how. The first thing I learned to make was oatmeal. The second was macaroni and cheese, with a sauce that sometimes involved a can of condensed cream of mushroom soup (I liked it that way) and sometimes didn't (the rest of the family preferred it without).

I don't remember wanting to learn to do the laundry, but my mother taught me (and my brothers and sister) to do that, too: sorting, washing, drying, folding, ironing. One of my brothers got so good at folding that when he was in college, little old ladies would gather around him at the laundromat for the pleasure of watching him fold his shirts.

My mother wasn't much on cleaning, so I mostly figured that out on my own. Perhaps this relatively late start on the cleaning front is why I have never attained (or, truth be told, aspired to) any particularly high standard of cleanliness. But by the time I was in my late twenties, I had spent years rather happily keeping house for myself and for other people, aware that this was not very fashionable but not really caring, because I liked it and on some level sensed the value of it, even if I didn't think about it very deeply.

My adventures in housework became more intense, however, during the years of my first marriage. I married my first husband at the end of my first year in graduate school and buried him four years later, at the beginning of my sixth year. Over the intervening years his worsening illness absorbed more and more of my energy, until in the last few months of his life I could do little more than moan to my therapist, "I can't cope; I can't cope; I can hardly get to the grocery store."

I understood then, with a clarity that I have experienced at few other times in my life, that getting to the grocery store was one of the things that Really Mattered. The dissertation could wait; dinner could not. Forget all the abstruse theological ideas that my classmates and teachers seemed to debate with such verve in the graduate seminars I was attending. Forget fantasies of "accomplishing something." Perhaps somewhere in the world there were people who measured their days by how much they got done—at work, in class, wherever. I measured my days by whether, at the end of them, the members of my household had been dressed and fed and bathed and put to bed. If we had been, then that was a good day. I had done what mattered most. Everything else was gravy.

As I moved in subsequent years through widowhood into a second marriage and, eventually, into motherhood, my practice of housekeeping changed to accommodate the changes in my household. But I retained the long-held sense, of which I had been made so consciously aware during those difficult years of illness, that housekeeping—cooking, cleaning, laundry, all the large and small tasks that go into keeping a household humming along—was not a trivial matter but a serious one. People need to eat, to sleep, to have clothes to wear; they need a place to read, a place to play, a place into which to welcome guests and from which to go forth into the world. These are the needs that housework exists to meet. Good academic and theologian that I was, I wondered, "Where are the books about this? Where are the books that might describe and unpack and explore the significance—both practical and spiritual—of this kind of work?"

I couldn't find many. The more I thought about it, the odder it seemed. After all, Jesus has very strong things to say at various points in the Gospels about the Christian duty to feed the hungry, clothe the naked, and shelter the homeless. He even goes so far, in his parable of the Last Judgment, as to paint this as the criterion by which the sheep are separated from the goats: "Come, O blessed of my Father, inherit the kingdom prepared for you from the foundation of the world; for I was hungry and you gave me food, I was thirsty and you gave me drink, I was a stranger and you welcomed me, I was naked and you clothed me, I was sick and you visited me.... Truly, I say to you, as you did it to one of the least of these my brethren, you did it to me" (Matthew 25:34–40).

There is a tendency, I think, on the part of those of us who are well fed, clothed, and housed to imagine that the needy people to whom Jesus refers in Matthew 25 are people we don't know—the sort of people who are served at homeless shelters and soup kitchens, at which we ought therefore to volunteer at least occasionally. But housework is all about feeding and clothing and sheltering people who, in the absence of that daily work, would otherwise be hungry and ill-clad and ill-housed.

There is undoubtedly more to the merciful service that Jesus describes in Matthew 25 than caring for the daily needs of the members of our own households. Housework is a beginning, not an end. But it is a beginning—not a sidetrack, not a distraction, but a beginning, and an essential one at that—in the properly Christian work of, among other things, meeting the everyday needs of others, whether those others be our fellow household members, our near neighbors, or people more sociologically or geographically distant from ourselves.

FANTASIES AND REALITIES

Housekeeping and domestic tasks in general have come to occupy a complex position in American popular culture. Odd as it would have seemed to my grandmother (who was a housewife all her adult life) or to my husband's grandmother (who did all her own housework and cleaned other people's houses for pay besides), housework is these days the subject of a great deal of fantasy. Designer cleaning products and accessories are marketed to high-end consumers who have no intention of cleaning their houses themselves (for that they have maids) but who like to imagine themselves waltzing about in sheer black aprons while wielding feather dusters. Newspapers bring us columns on fashion that feature haute couture–clad models striking poses on washing machines, the presumed message of which is that you can be expensively dressed, impossibly thin, and dramatically photogenic, all while a load of towels spins dry. Thirty-something women explain their plans to leave paid employment at some indefinite time in the future: "Home will be a total haven. I'll go through a stack of Martha Stewart books and learn to cook. I'll *feng shui* my furniture and pick just the right sheets from Garnet Hill. Keeping house sounds like fun."

Fun, that is, as opposed to work. Domesticity, we are to believe, is a leisure activity, one that results in elaborate, spotless perfection while requiring nothing of us but that we purchase a few brand-name products or publications. "Have the best of everything," coos an ad for one domesticity magazine. "Scatter seeds with your own hands. Pick perfect cherries. Take a nap in an orchard. Lift corn from the earth. Curl up with a kitty. Step into your garden. Make a wreath of ginger cookies. Belly flop on snow. Send in the postpaid card . . ." The message is clear: keeping house is not about mastering a set of complex and worthwhile skills for the sake of doing a good job at something that needs to be done. It is about being perfect without even trying. Just subscribe to this magazine, and your house—and your life—will be perfect.

The reality, of course, is that housekeeping is not effortless, and it is never perfect, even when it gets done, which happens less and less. Interest in housekeeping-as-fantasy appears actually to be rising more or less in proportion to decline in the actual doing of housework. Sociologists have found that over the past thirty or forty years, the amount of time that women spend doing housework has fallen by nearly half, with no comparable rise in the amount of time spent on housework by men. Food industry groups report that an ever-increasing percentage of meals are prepared or eaten (or both) away from home. When people do cook at home, they spend less time at it. They spend less time on laundry, too (they've given up ironing), and on cleaning (they've given up washing floors).

And housework of all kinds is increasingly relegated to the fringes of lives filled with other things. In her book *The Time Bind,* the sociologist Arlie Hochschild documents the increasing prevalence of homes in which every adult member of the household works full time for pay outside the home and no one bears explicit, dedicated responsibility—even part time—for tasks inside the home. The result, she says, is homes so chaotic and unstructured that all the adults in the household would rather be at work than at home. After all, at work people know what their jobs are and can take a break when they're done; at home all anyone knows is that it is a mess waiting for someone to clean it up.

The resentment and anger that this engenders in both men and women is evident in, among other places, a pair of edited volumes with marvelously evocative titles: *The Bitch in the House* and *The Bastard on the Couch*. These books, which purport to give women's and men's perspectives, respectively, on relationships, marriage, sex, and parenthood, turn out to be about housework as much as they are about anything else. Who is doing the housework? Who is not doing it? Who thinks someone else should be doing it, or at least doing more of it, more reliably, more cheerfully, more efficiently? Who is taking responsibility or shirking responsibility? Who feels overburdened and unappreciated? Who feels just plain overwhelmed and exhausted with the demands imposed, most often, by children, who seem constantly to be hungry, dirty, and making a mess?

And it is not just sophisticated, literate professionals with small children who are angry about housework. Parents of grown children who return home after having been away at college discover that in the middle of the night food disappears from the refrigerator and dirty dishes appear in the sink, and the next day no one offers to help with the marketing or the washing up. Retired men whose wives continue (or begin) to work outside the home are startled and dismayed to find that now they are expected to shoulder the majority of the housework, or at least more of it than they have been accustomed to doing. They resent their wives' expectations, and their wives resent their resistance. Young people, whether married or single, find themselves wishing the whole problem of housework would just go away. "We were both working," said one friend of mine, remembering the years before he and his wife had children, "and we both just wanted someone to take care of us."

This note of longing is the other side of the frazzled reality that is housework for many people. Shouldn't home be a place of refreshment, of nurturance, of beauty? Why do the house, and the housework, seem so out of control? Isn't there a better way? There are books speaking to these concerns, too. Their ostensible subjects range from the secular gospel of decluttering to the spiritual promise of inner healing, but their messages are remarkably similar: if you want to get your life in order, start with your house. Promises that women who declutter their homes will then inevitably lose weight are not uncommon. Renewed family lives, better financial positions, newfound purpose, peace, "blessing," and so forth are similarly portrayed as probable consequences of doing a better job with the housework.

Housekeeping, in other words, may be mundane, but it is not simple. It occupies territory characterized by strong and conflicting currents, from the visions of effortless perfection purveyed by the various divas of domesticity through the harried neglect documented by sociologists and the simmering resentment chronicled by legions of fiction and nonfiction writers to the simultaneously wistful and desperate longing for better things reflected in the housekeeping self-help literature. And then there is the question raised by a friend of mine who has been keeping house more or less faithfully, more or less cheerfully, for her husband and four children for more years than she cares to remember: "What's in it for me?"

THE ORIGINS OF HOUSEWORK

How has housekeeping come to occupy so conflicted a place, in both reality and imagination, in the lives of so many people? Part of the story is to be found in the process of industrialization, which in this country occurred over the course of the later nineteenth and earlier twentieth centuries and was accompanied by the separation of work into "public" and "private" spheres and the assignment—more complete in ideology than in fact—of "men's work" to the public sphere and "women's work" to the private sphere.

One effect of industrialization was that it virtually created the kind of work that we now call "housework." Before the mid-nineteenth century, the English word *housework* did not exist. What did exist were the words *housewifery* and *husbandry,* which since the Middle Ages had described the women's work and the men's work, respectively, that was required to run an agrarian household of the kind that became typical of the middle classes—people who were neither aristocrats governing large households employing and sheltering dozens or hundreds of individuals nor people laboring in the homes and on the farms of others, but married couples working their own land and supporting their own (relatively) small households. As the historian Ruth Schwartz Cowan observes, the word *housework* would probably have made no sense to anyone prior to industrialization "since—with the exception of seamen, miners, soldiers, and peddlers—almost all people worked in or on the grounds of a house, their own, or someone else's."

The process of industrialization, in separating work places from home places and identifying the former as a man's place and the latter as a woman's place, so altered the work of women (and in particular of married women) that a new word was required to describe it: *housework*. Before industrialization, women and men had worked together in and around the home at complementary unpaid tasks that were differentiated by gender: cutting and carrying wood (for men), building and tending fires (for women), making lye (for men), making soap (for women). After industrialization, men (and some women, mostly single) "went to work"—that is, they left their homes in order to labor somewhere else for wages, doing tasks that had been removed from the home to factories or other workplaces. Women (especially wives) "stayed home"—that is, they labored at home without pay, doing housework.

Postindustrial housework was in many instances quite different from the housewifery of the preindustrial era. Running water, refrigeration, gas and electric stoves, washing machines, commercially available soaps and detergents— these and other changes in household technology dramatically changed domestic labor by, among other things, enabling an individual housewife, at least if she worked hard and fast enough, to perform for her household as much or more work as had previously been required of two or three adult women (that is, the preindustrial housewife and her hired help). Industrialization, in other words, did not eliminate or even reduce women's work; what it did was vastly increase the productivity of women working at home.

And there was more work to do than ever. In the preindustrial household, articles of clothing were few and were laundered seldom, if ever. In the industrialized household, factory-made cotton clothing abounded and needed frequent washing (and bleaching and starching and ironing). The one-pot meals that simmered untended on the preindustrial hearth gave way to menus consisting of multiple dishes requiring active preparation on a stove. The arrival of indoor plumbing created a brand-new domestic chore: cleaning the bathroom, which with the advent of the germ theory of disease was recognized increasingly as absolutely essential for the health of the household. And all this work was to be done by the housewife by herself. Who was left at home to help her? Not her husband, who now went out to work somewhere else and was no longer available to assist with the heavy work in the middle of the day. Not the "hired girl," either, as she could now take a job at the mill and did not have to enter domestic service. The labor of running the industrialized household belonged to the housewife and the housewife alone.

Along with the development of industrialization and the accompanying notion of public and private spheres, however, went the widespread assumption that "real" work takes place in the public sphere and that whatever housewives do at home therefore cannot be work. Men (and single women, like the hired-girl-turned-millworker) worked in the public sphere, where they earned the money required for the purchase of goods and services in the industrialized economy. Married women worked at home, where they did, well, what? Men weren't sure. What did their wives do all day, anyway? Even housewives wondered. Here they were, surrounded by modern tools like stoves and washing machines that were supposed to liberate them from "drudgery"—so why were they perpetually exhausted?

The "problem" of housework thus became not just that it was "women's work" or that it was low-status but that it was widely suspected of not being work at all, even by the men who benefited directly from it and by the women whose lives were consumed by it. The seemingly endless amounts of work actually involved in housework (whose pace and quantity only increased with the introduction of every new laborsaving device), the absence of any help at home, and the lack of any recognition of the value and necessity—or even the reality—of the housewife's work surely went a long way toward fueling the fires of feminist theorizing about housework. For many feminists, the "housewife" embodied the very antithesis of the self-actualized human being. Germaine Greer, in *The Female Eunuch,* characterized the life of the full-time housewife as one of absolute servitude. Housewives, she said, "represent the most oppressed class of life—contracted unpaid workers, for whom slaves is not too melodramatic a description."

The feminist movement is nearly half a century old, and a lot of water has gone under the bridge. Many professions previously open only to men are now open to women, and women, including married women with children, are employed outside the home in record numbers. And many households and individuals now no longer operate under the assumption that household work "has to be done," at least not by anyone who is a member of the household. Gone are the days in which, as one former housewife remembers, "take-out or carry-home food was strictly for bachelors, and a frozen dinner, prepared by the hands of strangers, was reserved for times of crisis and regarded by the children as a rare treat and by the adults as a shiftless abdication of responsibility." Nowadays, take-out or carry-home has become the norm in many households and is regarded by many people as a simple necessity. After all, who has time to cook?

In fact, anyone who takes too much time to cook (or clean or iron) runs the risk of being regarded as a parasitic blot on society. One study on attitudes toward gender and the workplace found that "while 'business women' were rated as similar in competence to 'business men' and 'millionaires,' 'housewives' were rated as similar in competence to the 'elderly,' 'blind,' 'retarded,' and 'disabled.'" Attitudes like these appear not to reflect gender bias pure and simple, for if they did, businesswomen would presumably rank lower than businessmen. They appear, on the contrary, to be a reflection of judgments about housewives as such. I have a friend, a housewife, who says she cringes every time she fills out a form and is asked to state her occupation. Is it any wonder why?

DIVINE DOMESTICITY

What would happen if we were to look at housework and the doers of housework (whether "housewives" or not) not through the postindustrial and postfeminist lenses provided to us by our culture but through the lens of Christian scripture? What we would find is that God does not appear to think as lowly of housework and housekeepers as members of our culture are apt to. On the contrary, scripture abounds with images of God himself as homemaker and housedweller, as one who clothes and is clothed, who feeds people and animals and the earth itself and receives gifts of food and drink in return.

Consider Psalm 104:

> Thou . . . coverest thyself with light as with a garment,
> who hast stretched out the heavens like a tent, who hast
> laid the beams of thy chambers on the waters. . . . Thou
> didst set the earth on its foundations, so that it should
> never be shaken. Thou didst cover it with the deep as
> with a garment. . . . Thou makest springs gush forth in
> the valleys; they flow between the hills, they give drink
> to every beast of the field. . . . [All creatures] look to

thee, to give them their food in due season. When thou
givest to them, they gather it up; when thou openest
thy hand, they are filled with good things [vv. 1–2, 5–6,
10–11, 27–28].

The psalmist's portrayal is of God as a great housekeeper,
pitching a tent, clothing himself with light and the earth with
water as with garments, ordering boundaries, making homes
for creatures, giving them food, sustaining all life, creating and
re-creating through the Spirit.

These themes echo the creation stories of Genesis, in
which God sets the first humans in a home he had made for
them, a garden both beautiful and nourishing, for in it grew
"every tree that is pleasant to the sight and good for food"
(Genesis 2:9). When our first parents are expelled from the
garden, God's parting gesture is to clothe them (Genesis
3:21). And God continues to feed and clothe and shelter his
people even in their exile from Paradise: he rains bread from
heaven as they wander in the wilderness (Exodus 16:4), he
preserves their clothing (Deuteronomy 8:4), and he houses
them in booths (Leviticus 23:43).

God's own presence with his people is mediated through
dwelling places and domestic activities. In the book of Genesis we read of how the Lord appeared to Abraham as he sat
at the door of his tent beside the oaks of Mamre. God's ap-
pearing took the form of a visit from three strangers whom
Abraham and Sarah welcomed by preparing and serving a
meal of bread and meat and curds, and as they welcomed
these strangers they welcomed God himself and became recipients of God's promise and blessing (Genesis 18).

When the children of Israel are wandering in the wilderness, God meets with them all in another tent. The "tent of
meeting" is staffed by priests whose duties resemble in many

respects the work involved in keeping house: arranging coverings, putting out dishes and food, setting out lamps, arranging utensils and vessels, clearing away ashes (Numbers 4:4–14).

Eventually, the people of Israel settle down, and God settles down too, moving from tent to house, from tabernacle to temple. God does not "dwell" in his house in any grossly physical sense, as King Solomon acknowledges in the prayer with which he dedicates the temple (1 Kings 8:27–28), and yet God is particularly present to his people there. Prayers and petitions are properly brought to God at his house; forgiveness and healing and justice are properly expected from God there. And all these things happen in the context of the ongoing priestly service of God in the temple: the cleansing of vessels, the lighting of lamps, the offering of sacrifices, the preparation and serving of feasts.

When in the fullness of time God does come bodily to dwell with humans in the person of the incarnate Christ, he does so in a way reminiscent of his presence with the Israelites in their wanderings: "The Word became flesh, and pitched his tent among us," testifies John the Evangelist (John 1:14). Jesus describes himself as one who has "no place to lay his head," but he nonetheless shows himself remarkably conversant with the details of housekeeping. He speaks in parables about houses and householders, about sweeping and lamplighting, about vessels that appear clean on the outside but are soiled within. He enters the homes of others to eat with them and concerns himself with others' meals, as, for example, a little girl whom he heals: "Give her something to eat," he tells her parents (Mark 5:43).

At the same time, Jesus is far from exalting domesticity as the highest possible form of anyone's service to God or one's fellow human beings. In the well-known story of Jesus' visit to the home of Mary and Martha of Bethany, Mary sits at Jesus' feet and listens to his teaching while Martha busies herself in the kitchen preparing a meal for Jesus and his entourage (Luke 10:38–42). Finally, Martha goes to Jesus to complain that Mary is not helping her: "Lord, do you not care that my sister has left me to serve alone? Tell her then to help me."

Jesus' response is as notable for what he does not say as for what he does say. He does not shoo Mary into the kitchen. He does not commend Martha for her single-minded focus on domestic matters. Instead, he treats Martha with the same perplexing seriousness with which he treats other disciples and would-be disciples. "Martha, Martha, you are troubled about many things; one thing is needful. Mary has chosen the good portion, which shall not be taken away from her."

This exchange is more than a little reminiscent of a conversation recorded earlier in the gospel of Luke, in which Jesus invites a man to follow him and the man asks for permission first to bury his father. "Leave the dead to bury their own dead; but as for you, go and proclaim the kingdom of God" (Luke 9:60). It was unthinkable in that culture that a son should neglect the duty to bury his parents, and Jesus' words to this man pose a startling challenge to standard assumptions about what comes first. It was equally unthinkable in that culture that anyone should neglect to feed the hungry stranger at her door. Jesus' words to Martha are equally startling.

It appears that in Jesus' judgment, even so obviously necessary and pious an activity as burying one's parents takes second place to following Jesus. And even something so sacred as hospitality—the moral duty to welcome the stranger—takes second place relative to listening to Jesus' teaching. The first commandment (to love God with all one's heart and soul and strength and mind) always takes precedence over the second commandment (to love one's neighbor as oneself). But in the paradoxical realm that is real life, it is not possible to love God without loving neighbor, and a primary and essential way of loving one's neighbors is to feed and clothe and house them.

In fact, says Jesus, feeding the hungry and clothing the naked amount to performing the same services for Jesus himself (Matthew 25:40). Jesus is served not as people abandon prosaic duties like these but as people perform such duties. And Jesus portrays a future hope that suggests the activities involved in making a home stand not in contrast to but in continuity with Jesus' own redemptive work. "In my Father's house are many rooms," he assures his disciples (John 14:2). "If someone loves me, he will keep my word, and my Father will love him, and we will come to him and make our home with him" (John 14:23).

The "homely" character of redemption is, in fact, one of the overarching themes of scripture. God leads the people of Israel into a promised land whose blessings are envisioned as homes to dwell in, clothes to wear, food and drink to satisfy hunger and thirst. The prophetic hope in the midst of homes despoiled is of "a peaceful habitation, secure dwellings, quiet resting places" (Isaiah 32:18). Jesus speaks of the kingdom of God as a banquet at which God is determined every seat should be filled (Luke 14:23). Paul envisions redemption in terms of finally being fully clothed (2 Corinthians 5:4). The book of Revelation offers an eschatological hope that consists in a well-ordered and beautiful city in which God himself dwells with his people (Revelation 21).

The Christian story of redemption, in other words, is a story that moves from home to home. The journey from Eden to the New Jerusalem is one that is characterized by exile and pilgrimage, to be sure, but also by shelter on the way. Such shelter is necessary for creatures like ourselves, not just for our bodies but for our whole selves. What man or woman or child can remember Eden or long for Jerusalem who has never had any temporal home at all? The practicalities of housekeeping—cooking, cleaning, laundry—are among the things that ground our existence in the particular times and places in which we live and in so doing make it possible for us to keep alive the memory of our first home in paradise and the hope of our ultimate home in God's new creation.

THE LITANY OF EVERYDAY LIFE

Precisely because human beings are both physical and spiritual beings, even so profoundly physical a discipline as housekeeping has a spiritual dimension. Perhaps it is not surprising, therefore, that the popular culture of domesticity, far from being a secular realm, is instead suffused with spiritual language that is used to describe both the challenges of housekeeping and their solution. Cable television hosts exhort viewers to "exorcise homes of their sinful mess." Authors of housekeeping manuals suggest that we "clear our clutter with *feng shui*," that we discover the "joy of Zen" as we sweep our floors, that we feel "God breezes" as we go about our cleaning routines. Our ambivalent and conflicted practices with respect to domestic matters appear to be felt in the collective soul of our culture as a kind of crisis, one that cries out to be addressed in specifically, if not exclusively, spiritual terms.

The problem with many spiritualities of housekeeping is that the remedy they prescribe amounts to more of the disease. Consider the suggestion offered by a magazine devoted to "simplicity" in domestic matters: "This is the month to buy that luggage or 32-inch TV you've been eyeing—and denying yourself—for years." The reader's problem, as this magazine sees it, is self-denial, and the solution is a 32-inch television set. We are just not good enough consumers, but with a little guidance we can get better, which will come as a great relief to us.

A good deal of the housekeeping literature, in fact, functions as a kind of spiritualized therapy for the anxiety brought on by materialism. "Simplicity" has become the promised land, and "decluttering" the religious practice par excellence. The one thing this gospel does not call into question is the underlying assumption that it is both possible and desirable to be it all, have it all, and do it all. On the contrary: "Our reader is overworked, overcommitted, and oversched-uled," says the publisher of the same magazine. "She loves her life and has way too much on her plate, but she doesn't want to give any of it up."

If we are honest, we will recognize this for the decep-tion that it is. If we are feeling the ill effects of being spread half an inch thick and going a million miles an hour, the solu-tion is not to go ever faster and be spread ever thinner. The solution is to take a deep breath, identify what really matters, and do more of that and less of other things.

So what really matters? Well, housework, among other things. It is not the only thing that matters, but it does matter. It matters that people have somewhere to come home to and that there be beds and meals and space and order available there. Whether we do a lot of housework or a little of it, whether we keep house only for ourselves or for other people as well, housework forms part of the basic patterning of our lives, a pattern that we might identify as a kind of "litany of everyday life."

A litany, as Christians have traditionally understood it, is a form of prayer that includes the announcement of various needs or requests, each followed by a response like "Amen" or "Lord, have mercy." Litanies have long been popular among laypeople, who have found in their structure and flexibility a way to pray that speaks to their concerns in tangible and accessible ways. Litanies tend to be both repetitive and comprehensive, and in both of these characteristics there is a certain analogy to housework.

A litany is typically about a lot of different things; it includes requests for God's assistance or care on many different fronts at once. In so doing, a litany draws together the disparate threads of our needs and our concerns and tempers their potentially overwhelming nature. When we have prayed through a litany, we may not have prayed at great length about everything of concern to us, but at least we have covered the bases.

Housework, too, is about a lot of different things. There are errands to be run, meals to be planned, clothes to be laundered, messes to be dealt with. It doesn't take very much disorganization before you feel that you have been trying to juggle a dozen balls and they are all coming crashing down around you. But there is a fundamental unity and focus to housework, too: it is about a certain number of basic needs, and if you are addressing those needs—if, over the course of the day and week and year, the members of your household get dressed and fed and bathed and put to bed—then you can know you have done the things that matter most.

Housework is repetitive, as well. You cannot pick up a room once and be done with it forever. Every time you cook a meal, it disappears shortly thereafter; a few hours later, everyone is hungry again. Clothes laundered today will be in the hamper tomorrow. Anyone who keeps house may on occasion be tempted to throw up his or her hands and declare with Simone de Beauvoir, "Few tasks are more like the torture of Sisyphus than housework, with its endless repetition."

At such moments we do well to listen instead to the philosopher Søren Kierkegaard: "Repetition is the daily bread that satisfies with benediction." Granted, Simone de Beauvoir probably did more housework in her day than Kierkegaard did in his. But repetition, in itself, is not equivalent to oppressive futility. The sun comes up every morning. Christians gather every Sunday to celebrate the resurrection of Jesus from the dead. Every year brings the cycle of the seasons and of the Christian calendar: Advent, Christmas, Epiphany, Lent, Eastertide, Pentecost, Ordinary Time.

Housework is akin to these natural and human rhythms of the day, the week, the year. We fix lunch because it is lunchtime. We wash the clothes or the windows because it is Monday or because it is sunny. We pack away coats and boots and get out shorts and sleeveless shirts because winter is over and summer is coming. As we engage with the litany of everyday life, we engage with life itself, with our fellow human beings, with the world in which God has set us all, and thus with God himself.

The particular form this litany takes will look different for different people at different times. There is no one right way to keep house, for so much depends on who is doing the housework, for whom, and under what circumstances. But housekeeping is part of a tradition that takes seriously the basic, homely needs of people for food and clothing and shelter. These are needs that God takes seriously and that Jesus encourages Christians to take seriously. They are not the only important things in the world. But they are important; they have an intrinsic significance and worth that is too often lost amid the busyness and the technological background noise of the modern world.

My own house and my housekeeping are works in progress, and sometimes it seems that very little progress is actually being made. But I can only imagine the chaos into which my household would long ago have descended if I were less intentional about making time to keep house and if I were less convinced of the inherent value of doing so. We all need the patterns of our lives to echo and emulate the patterns of the larger story that we, as Christians, believe is the true story of the world. Daily involvement in the work of housekeeping, the litany of everyday life, is one way of participating in and living out that story.

A Place to Live

One of the most fundamental of human longings is the longing for home. We long for a place that feels like the right place, where we belong, where we ourselves are longed for and welcomed. And for all its spiritual and psychological dimensions, this longing is physical and material as well. We want there to be a place where waiting for us are a room, a bed, a chair, a meal—the things that meet the basic needs of embodied beings like ourselves. We want "the comforts of home," not just somewhere away from home—a fancy hotel, say—but at home, where, we sense, they are supposed to be.

Christian scripture presents these needs and longings as an intrinsic and positive aspect of human experience. When God created our first parents, we are told, he set them in a home that he had made for them, one that was beautiful to look at and full of good things to eat, where the work of tilling and tending the garden yielded a ready harvest of plenty. The tragedy of the sin of Adam and Eve, in the wake of which they were expelled from that beautiful, God-given place, was not only that their friendship with God was spoiled; it was that they lost their home, exchanging the beauty and fruitfulness of Eden for the bitter and hostile harshness of the

wilderness. Home, once an encompassing reality, was now re-
duced to dim memory and distant longing.

As the story of redemption unfolds in scripture, again
and again the grace of God is directed toward two inter-
woven purposes: restoring humans' friendship with God and
in the process bringing people home. God calls Abraham out
of Ur in order to give him and his descendants a home in the
Promised Land. The songs of the prophets and the psalmists
portray home as God's present and future gift. "Thou pre-
parest a table before me in the presence of my enemies," says
David. "Thou makest me lie down beside quiet waters"
(Psalm 23:2, 5). One day, says the prophet Isaiah, God's Spirit
will finally be poured out and God's people "will abide in a
peaceful habitation, in secure dwellings, and in quiet resting
places" (32:18). The eventual inclusion of the gentiles in
God's redemptive plan, says the apostle Paul, involves bringing them home to dwell together with the children of Abraham in God's own household: "You are no longer strangers
and sojourners, but you are fellow citizens with the saints and
members of the household of God" (Ephesians 2:19).

There is another strand to the biblical portrayal of
home, however. The children of Israel spend many, many
years living in tents in the wilderness as they follow God's
leading from their exile in Egypt to the promise of home in
Canaan. Jesus points out to potential disciples that he has no
home: "Foxes have holes and birds of the air have nests; but
the Son of man has nowhere to lay his head" (Matthew 8:20).
Jesus' followers, say various New Testament authors, are to
remember that they too are citizens not of earth but of
heaven; all their earthly lives they will be strangers in a
strange land, and they will not truly come home until God
brings all things to their conclusion and new beginning in
the New Jerusalem (Philippians 3:20; 2 Peter 3:13).

This negative side of the biblical portrait of home has over the years tended to capture a good portion of Christian rhetoric and imagination. In the early centuries of the church, men (and a few women) left their homes to dwell in the harshness of the desert, thinking that God was more likely to be encountered there than at home. The medieval theologian Hugh of Saint Cher (who had himself left home for the alternative community of the cloister) opined that "the man who finds his homeland sweet is still a tender beginner; he to whom every soil is as his native one is already strong; but he is perfect to whom the entire world is a foreign place."

In a time nearer to our own, we find cultural critics like Malcolm Muggeridge echoing such sentiments, declaring that "the only ultimate disaster that can befall us [Christians] is to feel ourselves to be at home here on earth. As long as we are aliens we cannot forget our true homeland, which is that other kingdom [Jesus] proclaimed." Christians are admonished by various contemporary theologians to avoid the comfortable complacency of supposing that this world is our true home. We are, rather, to remember that God's people are always to be "resident aliens," people who yearn for the fulfillment of all things in God and cannot feel themselves at home until that day has come. We are to realize that the rootlessness many people feel arises from the fact that nowhere but heaven will ever fully satisfy the human longing for home.

It is certainly true that it is not a good thing to confuse earth with heaven, to mistake the old creation for the new creation, to prefer the status quo to God's transforming gift. We don't want to imitate the Israelites in their attachment to the comfort of life in Egypt and their consequent lack of enthusiasm for the journey into the Promised Land. We don't want to be so set on making or finding the "perfect" home here and now that we neglect to hope for the home that God is preparing for all his people in the fullness of time.

But home is not just an eschatological expectation, not just an existential category, not just the object of our deepest longing. Home is a practical, daily reality. Even resident aliens need a place to cook and eat their meals, to put away their clothes, to lie down to sleep at night and wake up in the morning. Scripture suggests that God cares about those things. They are, or at least they can be, part of the day-to-day working out of God's redemptive activity in the lives of individuals and in the world.

WHAT IS A HOME?

In contemporary America, a dominant cultural image of home is that of refuge. Images of home as refuge arose in the nineteenth century in the course of industrialization as certain kinds of work were removed from the home and relocated to factories, where time clocks, paychecks, and—often—inhumanely long hours made entirely understandable the longing for some place of retreat from the dehumanizing pressures of the marketplace. The preindustrial home had itself been a workplace, but in the industrialized world, home became a haven from the relentless demands for practicality and production imposed by assembly lines and marketing campaigns.

Thus today we find recommendations on "how to make a house a home" that make sense only if we assume that home is a place where impracticality reigns supreme. The authors of one home advice book suggest lighting one's kitchen exclusively with lamps fitted with 7½-watt appliance bulbs. What are they thinking? You are supposed to cook in the dark? But of course that is not the point; the point is that "home" is to be a soft and gentle place, a refuge from the harsh and glaring lights of early-twenty-first-century American society.

In a more positive vein, we find affirmations that home is to be a place of self-expression and self-actualization. This again owes a good deal to the demands of the industrialized workplace that individuals subsume their own talents and imaginations to the dictates of the market. A craftsman could—and commonly did—make every wagon, every shoe, every clock an individualized work of art. An assembly-line worker has to make every widget exactly the same and to someone else's specifications. Where, then, to exercise one's talents and creativity? At home. Interior decorating magazines thus offer quizzes meant to identify an individual's "style" and then prescribe advice tailored specifically to particular styles, along with lists of products that people can buy to express those styles.

These ways of thinking of home—as a refuge from the marketplace and as a setting for the development and display of one's inner self—are so deeply ingrained in our common cultural mind-set that it can be difficult to imagine home in any other terms. This is true even for Christians, who often retain some sense that there is something theologically significant about home, but in their effort to express that sense can manage to do little more than enter with pious enthusiasm into these common cultural conceptions. A friend of mine relates a story about a number of women of her acquaintance, all of whom were stay-at-home mothers and the wives of wealthy men and devoted a good deal of time and money to the regular redecoration of their homes. When asked whether this was necessarily the best use of all these resources, the women replied, "But that's what a good Christian wife does—make a beautiful home for her family."

These women were right in their central contention: making a beautiful, comfortable home is a Christian thing to do. But what that involves is not necessarily the same as throwing oneself headlong into the world of upscale decorating magazines. Making a home involves constructing and maintaining an environment in which people can flourish in ways in which God desires for people to flourish. Four images, each of them rooted in Christian scripture and tradition, suggest themselves as ways in which Christians can picture what home is for and thus some of what might be involved in making a home.

In the first place, a home is an inn. An inn is a place where a traveler can find a meal and shelter for the night, usually in the company of other travelers. It is a modest sort of place, offering simple accommodations to people of modest means and with normal, foreseeable human needs. Joseph and Mary sought shelter at an inn when Mary's time of delivery drew near. The Good Samaritan took the man who had fallen among thieves to an inn, where he cared for the man. So also should a home be a place where it is safe to be when you are hungry or tired—or sick or a new parent or newly born yourself, for that matter—because meals and beds and the care that goes with them are available there as a matter of course.

A home is also a sanctuary. A sanctuary is a place set apart for encounter, whose separateness exists for the sake of relationship. When God led the people of Israel out of Egypt, he commanded them to build him a sanctuary so that he could dwell in their midst. The psalmist sings of entering the sanctuary of God and having his despair turn to confidence as he encounters God and God's renewing comfort. A sanctuary, in other words, is not a cocoon whose inhabitants dwell in splendid, impenetrable isolation. A sanctuary has boundaries that are meant to be crossed. A home likewise should be a place with a door that can be opened or closed, a place whose very separateness serves to foster relationship both within and across its boundaries.

A home is a city. Again and again in scripture we find God's desires for human flourishing expressed in terms of a city, from the earthly Jerusalem of prophet and psalmist to the heavenly Jerusalem of the book of Revelation. A city is an active place; there are a lot of people there, and they are busy with a lot of things. A city is thus very different from a suburb, the central notion of which involves getting away from other people and the everyday commotion of urban life. Often we can be surprised when running a household involves more or less continuous activity. We shouldn't be. The life of a city ebbs and flows with the hour and the season, but it never ceases altogether; so it is with the life of a home.

And finally, a home is a castle. When scripture describes the dwelling places that God designs for himself and for humans, it does so in terms that call to mind the rich, ceremonious beauty of a castle with all its pomp and pageantry: the tabernacle, with all its rich fabrics and woods, the jewel-encrusted New Jerusalem. This kind of labor-intensive richness is out of fashion nowadays; we want everything to be quick and easy, or we think we do. But there is something in the human soul that longs for beauty beyond necessity. Of course it is easier not to make the bed. But there is a substantive difference between turning down a neatly made bed in the evening and lying down in a mess of sheets left from the night before. To be beautiful, a home need not be luxurious in size or in contents. The beauty of a well-kept home may arise simply from structure and ritual and attention to detail, things that can be present even in the most modest of homes.

WHO MAKES A HOUSEHOLD?

There is a tendency on the part of many of us to assume that one keeps house for one's family and that marriage is the point at which one acquires a family. There was a day when getting married and setting up housekeeping really were the same thing for many people, when the majority of young people lived as members of their parents' households as long as they remained single. These days, the break from the parental household tends to come not with marriage but before it, with new milestones called "going away to college" or "getting the first apartment." These are now the points at which many people first set up housekeeping, in the sense that they begin to acquire a whole range of household-type accoutrements, from bedding to cooking equipment to clothes storage arrangements.

There remains, however, a lingering cultural suspicion that a real household, the kind that requires housekeeping, is a household with a marriage at its center. Consider the social ritual of the bridal shower. The typical bride and groom of today have been out of their parents' homes for years and have no need for household equipment; the challenge they face is how to dispose of their duplicate kitchen appliances. The people who really need showers are the people leaving their parents' homes for apartment or dormitory life, but do they get them? Not as long as they remain single. The operating assumption apparently is that as long as there is no marriage, there is no household and consequently no need for gifts of electric frying pans and sets of monogrammed towels.

Marriage is a good way to form a household, but it is far from the only way. And people do not suddenly need dinner on the table just because they have gotten married. People need dinner whether they are married or single, whether they live alone or with one friend or several, whether they have children or not, whether they are young or old or somewhere in between. Christians are accustomed to taking marriage seriously, as well they ought to be. But the category of the household is not equivalent to that of either marriage or family, and the disciplines involved in making a home are needed by all people, whatever the shape of their household arrangements.

Recent surveys have shown that there are now more single-person households in America than there are households that include parents and minor children. This dramatic rise in the number of people living alone is due in part to changes in household technology that have made it possible for one person both to earn a living and to do the work involved in making a home. My paternal grandfather, who was born in 1887, did not marry until he was in his mid-forties. He could have lived alone in the 1920s and 1930s only if he had had the means to hire servants to cook his meals and clean his house and wash his clothes. He did not have such means, and so he lived for eighteen years as a "paying guest" in the home of acquaintances who did have a cook and a maid and a laundress.

Nowadays, of course, a bachelor professor would just rent an apartment and do his own marketing and cooking and laundry after work. Or would he? The reality is that even with modern "conveniences" like automatic washing machines and microwave ovens and vacuum cleaners, keeping house is a lot of work. And with no one else around to complain about there being nothing to eat and nothing to wear, it can be all too easy for a person who lives alone to fall into habits that nurture neither body nor soul. A central challenge for the person who lives alone is to take himself or herself seriously, not just as an individual, but as a household of one. You may live alone, but you need routines of tidiness and mealtimes just as much as people who live with others do, both for your own sake and for the sake of any guests who may cross your threshold.

Even aside from people who live alone, the tendency in the modern world is for households to become smaller and smaller. The "nuclear family" consisting only of parents and minor children (and not many of those) contrasts sharply with the extended family clans that one meets in the pages of scripture and tradition. A family like Jacob's, with twelve sons and one daughter by two wives and two concubines, would be remarkable indeed at most Sunday school picnics. Even a more conventional (by our lights) household like Martin Luther's included not only his wife and their six children but also a large and shifting population of students and guests, all of whom lived and ate together in the old Augustinian cloister in Wittenberg. In many places in the world, extended-family living is still the norm, but for most modern Americans, smaller-scale arrangements prevail.

Smaller households tend to undergo much more dramatic change over time than larger households. A large household tends to include a broad range of people all of the time—there are always some old people, always some young people, always some people in between. A small household, by contrast, changes as much over time as the few individuals who comprise it do. There may in a small household be a few years in which there are young children and then many years in which there are none. Children can feel like an intrusion in such a household; parents may spend the preschool years waiting for things to "get back to normal." But young childhood is just as normal a state of life as adulthood; we just tend to forget that, in our age-segregated society. Keeping house in a smaller household calls for the flexibility necessary to see a variety of situations as "normal" and a willingness repeatedly to reassess the changing needs of household members and the varying contributions that household members can make to the work of the household.

In contrast to the modern trend for ever-smaller households stand those that go beyond the boundaries of the nuclear family. I think, for example, of my friend Shannon and her apartment mate, who while they were still college students took in an elementary-school-age foster son. I think of my friend Mary-Alice and her sister Nora, both of them single women, who live together along with Mary-Alice's adopted daughter. I think of several young couples of my acquaintance who have chosen to live in unconventional arrangements— two of the couples with each other in a household of four, the other couple in a "house of hospitality" that includes several people in rather marginal social situations (like being recently released from jail or a drug treatment facility).

In each of these cases, people who might have been expected to set up housekeeping separately have instead chosen to do so together. All of the impetus of the modern world is toward separateness; we think it is normal for people to be by themselves and make an exception, as it were, for spouses and young children. But the momentum in scripture is toward community, not separateness, and the bonds of community in scripture go well beyond those of the nuclear family. God sets not only married couples and their children in families but widows and orphans as well.

Communal household arrangements are one way of testifying to this community-creating aspect of God's work of redemption. Such households are not necessarily better than households that are more conventional, by the lights of the modern world, but neither are they second-best or inherently cumbersome and problematic. They are real households; there is real sustenance in their daily rhythms and in the relationships that are nurtured by those rhythms.

WHOSE JOB IS HOUSEWORK?

The development of housework from the housewifery of an earlier age meant that until a few decades ago, the nearly universal cultural assumption was that all work inside the home should be performed by women—or more specifically, by wives. In a famous essay titled "I Want a Wife," published in 1972 in the inaugural issue of *Ms.* magazine, the writer Judy Syfers—herself a wife—reflected on how convenient it would be to *have* a wife, someone who would launder the clothes and pick up the house, who would prepare nutritious meals for the children and elegant dinners for the adults, who would see to it that the household ran perfectly smoothly all of the time, all with no assistance or thanks from anyone. "My God," Syfers exclaims at the end of her essay, "who *wouldn't* want a wife?"

The alternative proposed by many feminists was that housework be shared by all members of the household, especially by husbands. This very reasonable suggestion was often inadvertently undermined by the accompanying assumption that housework is intrinsically unpleasant. The poem "Housework," written by the Broadway lyricist Sheldon Harnick and also published in an early issue of *Ms.,* makes this assumption explicit: "Your Mommy hates housework. Your Daddy hates housework. I hate housework, too. And

when you grow up, so will you." The solution to this supposedly universal hatred of housework? Husbands and wives
should share the burden, so no one gets stuck with all the
scut work.

Not surprisingly, this was a rallying cry that raised very
few troops. In response to the contention that everyone
hates housework, many people drew, and still draw, a different conclusion: no one should do it—no one with any
choice in the matter at least. Men needn't feel any compul-
sion to do housework since, after all, it is not (really) their
job. And middle-class women with options shouldn't do it
either, since they have so many better things to do with their
time. One household management consultant neatly sums
up these lines of thought in her book *A Housekeeper Is
Cheaper Than a Divorce*. Men, she says, simply don't care
about housework, so don't knock yourself out trying to get
your husband to share in it. Just hire someone else to do it,
and get on with your life.

The problem here should be obvious. If the smart thing
to do with respect to housework is to hand it off to someone
else, this says something about people who end up doing
the housework: they are laboring at work that is intrinsically
contemptible. It is a small step from regarding the work as contemptible to regarding the worker as contemptible. Add to this
the fact that paid domestic workers are almost all women,
many of them poor and brown-skinned and imported from
halfway around the world, and all of them working in non-
public spaces where it is easy to be mistreated and have no
witnesses and no recourse, and you have a recipe for injustice
at least as great as the taken-for-grantedness of housewives
and their labor that was so deplored by the contributors to
Ms. magazine and the rest of the feminist movement.

Precisely because housework is necessary, it is not contemptible. And there is nothing wrong with hiring out the housework, or various bits and pieces of it, any more than there is anything intrinsically wrong with buying shoes or electricity rather than trying to make them yourself. At its best, hiring out some of the housework can constitute an acknowledgment that you can't do it all yourself. I have a friend who lived for a number of years in Indonesia, where she had several helpers who worked full or part time in her home. When she moved back to the United States, she could only imagine the astonishment those helpers would have felt upon learning that she was doing all their jobs herself, in addition to earning a living and raising five children on her own. Of course, the children worked with her in making their home, but if she could have afforded to hire adult help as well, she would certainly have done so. Keeping house is a big job, and we all need help, at least on occasion.

On the other hand, there are good reasons for doing housework yourself, regardless of your gender or your station in life. Hiring out the housework can amount to a claim to being above daily manual labor, to being the sort of person who does only "important" things. One lifestyle magazine quotes a woman who said of a particular point in her life that she had decided from then on to spend as little time as possible "doing things that just don't matter." The result? "I haven't had my head inside a toilet since." I doubt, however, that this woman's toilet has gone uncleaned in the intervening years. I suspect that someone else has been cleaning it, someone whose role in life, her employer imagines, is to do work that "doesn't matter." We all need something in our lives that can keep us from going down this road, the road of imagining ourselves too important to work with our hands.

Housework, precisely because it is so daily and so present, is as good an opportunity as any.

The rhythms of housework also provide a way to resist the relentless 24/7 pace of modern life in favor of something more suited to human embodiment and relationality. New parents are sometimes dismayed to discover that babies and young children require predictability to thrive. Children need a sense of when it is time to wake up, time to eat, playtime, naptime, bathtime, bedtime. Their parents, on the other hand, have sometimes been under the impression, encouraged by our culture, that a good life is one in which you act on impulse, not on schedule. No wonder parenthood comes as a shock to them: not only are they new parents, but they are also new to the creation of the rhythms of home. How much more conducive to the well-being of the household it would be, both before and after children, if housework and housekeeping were treated as an intrinsic and positive part of life in the body and in community rather than as a set of boring and limiting chores imposed on you by parenthood.

Children themselves benefit from being made part of the team that does the housework. Children long for connection with the real things of the real world, for work that is real and satisfying and that can help them become creators and producers rather than simply spectators and consumers of the labor of others. When we take time to teach a child to crack an egg or set the table, when we allow a child to fold the laundry or wash the floor, when we respond to the contributions of children with appreciation rather than criticism, we encourage the child to see himself or herself as a worker and a contributor to the economy of the household.

Children are, or course, exquisitely sensitive to cultural messages, including messages about the value of housekeeping and domestic activities. Much of the time, these cultural messages are not positive. If we want our children to develop and enjoy competence in the practices that go into making a home, we will have to show them by our own example that these are things that really matter: they are worth doing, worth caring about, and worth handing on to the next generation.

GOD'S WORK AND OUR WORK

Somewhere along the line, many of us (helped along by Madison Avenue and Disneyland) have developed a kind of magical idealization of domesticity. Mirror, mirror on the wall, who is the best housekeeper of them all? The diva of domesticity, that's who. Sometimes the diva is Supermom; sometimes she is Alice from *The Brady Bunch*. Some of us want to be the diva; some of us want to employ the diva; others want to marry the diva.

Essential to the fantasy is the idea that what the diva of domesticity does is fundamentally mysterious. She waves her magic wand, and there it is—the spotless house, the gourmet meal, the perfectly organized closets full of perfectly pressed clothes. And the perfect family, perfect bank account, and perfect life to go with them.

Of course this is silly. But too many of us spend too much energy mourning the fact that our housekeeping is not magical when we would do better to think about what kind of work housekeeping is. Housework is not magic. Housework is work, and as such it has characteristics typical of many other kinds of work, including God's work.

To begin with, work is creative. God is the creator and has given to humans the dignity and privilege of imitating and thus participating in God's work as creator. Housework is a part of this. By this I do not mean that there are aspects of housework that are creative (making jelly, for example), in contrast to the aspects of housework that are not creative (chipping bubblegum off the bathroom rug). It has seemed this way to some people; as one former housewife complains, "There is janitorial housewifery and creative housewifery, and the creative is kind of fun but strictly optional these days, and if you do a lot of it you won't have any time for the janitorial part, which is not fun, or optional either."

On the contrary, all of housework is creative, including the so-called janitorial part of it. When God created the heavens and the earth, he started with chaos and ended with a finely differentiated and beautiful universe. Housework is all about bringing order out of chaos. That heap of damply repulsive clothes on the bathroom floor turns into stacks of neatly folded clean laundry in a matter of hours; a dining table piled high with junk mail, school papers, and forgotten socks turns into a table neatly set for a meal; a sack of potatoes, properly peeled, boiled, riced, and seasoned, turns into a dish of mashed potatoes that the individuals assembled around the table are happy to eat.

In a society dominated by its monetary economy, it is easy to assume that any unpaid activity is either a form of consumption or an oppressive waste of time. But housework, although unpaid (if you do your own), is essentially productive; it is among the ways in which humans can and do participate in God's own work of creation.

Work is also providential. God's creative activity did not issue in a creation that lives on indefinitely with no further involvement on God's part. On the contrary, the very creatureliness of the universe requires the continuing presence and activity of God in sustaining all things in being. We recognize this readily in certain spheres of human activity. Everyone knows that a garden, once planted, does not thrive without the continued work of the gardener in weeding, mulching, fertilizing, pruning, harvesting, and beginning the cycle again in the new year.

A home is not much different from a garden in this sense. If you don't take care of a house, it devolves. This is true of the physical structure itself—we have all felt a twinge of sadness on seeing the sagging porches and peeling paint of a house long abandoned. And it is true of the internal workings of the household as well. A household has to be tended if it is to flourish and grow. Housework is never "done" in the same sense that gardening is never done or that God's providential involvement in the world is never done. Housework and gardening and God's providence itself are exercises not in futility but in faithfulness—faithfulness to the work itself, to the people whose needs that work serves, and to the God whose own faithfulness invites our faithful response.

Work is also incarnational. When God comes to the aid of his sad and broken creation, he does so not in some abstract way, simply willing for people to be healed but keeping his distance from the messy reality of their lives. On the contrary, God comes to live among human beings as one of us, including all of our bodily messiness. Redemption is profoundly, essentially physical; the Jesus who shared, and shares, your humanity and mine lived and suffered and died on our behalf.

Housework, too, is essentially physical. Indeed, a complaint commonly lodged against housework is that it is "menial"—work for servants—in contrast to other, higher-status kinds of work that may not include getting one's hands dirty. But if in Jesus God himself could take up a towel and wash other people's feet, surely we, as Jesus' adopted brothers and sisters, can find it in us to wash one another's dirty clothes and dirty dishes and dirty floors. Active engagement with fundamentally physical practices like housekeeping can be a way of remembering that a properly human life is a life of service in and through the body. It was so for Jesus, and it is so for us.

Work is sacramental as well. In a traditional Christian understanding, sacraments are points at which material and spiritual things come together and God is present and active in particular ways. Christians usher new members into the church by baptizing them with water. Christian worship is centered on a meal of bread and wine. These physical objects and practices remind Christians of God's past and present faithfulness and undergird their hope for the future: the wedding supper of the Lamb, the new life with which God promises to clothe each of us.

Other practices, while not sacraments properly speaking, may in a similar way allow physical objects and actions to link believers to Christian memory, hope, and present faithfulness. The work involved in making a home can be such a practice. The provision of home is a central aspect of God's creative and redemptive activity. Housekeeping can provide a way of remembering, anticipating, and participating in the kind of home-providing work that God does.

All the more is this so when our homes are not all we might wish them to be. God's world is not as he wishes it to be either. But God is present and active, even in the midst of continuing imperfection and brokenness. Christians do well to cultivate a similarly mindful, hopeful faithfulness as they engage in the basic, necessary disciplines of feeding, clothing, and housing one another.

And finally, work requires sabbath. Even God rests; after his six days of creation, God rested on the seventh day, and he instructs his people likewise to rest from their labors from time to time. Too often we are inclined to do this, and to make it possible for others to do this, more in some cases than in others. We have all heard the saying "A man's work is from sun to sun; a woman's work is never done." This is a fundamental reason why so much of "women's work" is construed and experienced as drudgery—not simply because it is repetitive, not simply because it involves manual labor, but because it comes with no time off, ever.

Even now, in a culture in which it is commonly expected that both men and women will work for pay outside the home, some people (usually men) expect to come home from work to rest, and other people (usually women) are expected to come home from work to more work. It is certainly true that the needs that housework serves do not take a day off. Every day, people need to eat. Every day, they need clothes to wear, a roof over their heads, a floor that is clear enough to walk on. But this does not mean that it is one person's job to labor incessantly to provide these things for everybody else. Sharing the work of the household, for those of us who live in shared households, is a way of allowing all members of the household to keep sabbath, to rest from their labors even as God rests from his.

3

Sheltering a Household

Not long ago I was talking with a friend who was bringing me up to date on the details of his family's life. His parents no longer lived in the house in which they had raised him and his brothers. They had sold that property, bought some land, and built their dream house, where they were now enjoying their retirement.

It was only later that I found myself reflecting on that term, "dream house." The "dream house," whether as a goal attained or an object desired, is part of the currency of modern American culture. Checkout aisles are stocked with magazines featuring floor plans and decorating schemes for dream houses; television schedules are filled with programs about people whose houses have just been "made over" into dream houses.

What are these dream houses like? I haven't seen my friend's parents' house, so I can't speak to it, but the cultural ideal is of a house that is luxurious in style and in size. The dream house is full of space and full of things; it is spotless and in perfect order all the time, and it stays that way all by itself (or at least that appears to be the implication of that oft-repeated mantra, "low maintenance").

The ideal of the dream house is problematic on a number of levels. In real life, the more space and things you have, the more time and trouble it takes to keep them clean and tidy, no matter how many features of your house may be "low maintenance." And in real life, most people cannot afford the kind of luxurious surroundings that are simply taken for granted in the fantasy world of the dream house.

In the real world, many people struggle to afford any house at all. Advocacy groups like the National Coalition for the Homeless report a significant rise in homelessness over the past several decades, driven by a growing shortage of affordable housing and a simultaneous increase in poverty. The number of people living in substandard housing or who are precariously housed (who, for example, must spend so great a proportion of their income on housing that they are one paycheck away from eviction) is increasing as well.

The decrease in affordable housing is the flip side of rising housing values and the large-scale development of luxury housing. As housing prices rise, fewer people are able to afford to buy a home without recourse to risky mortgage arrangements. As urban apartments are converted to condominiums, tenants are left to scramble for the few rental units left. And as suburban communities give precedence to the development of large single-family detached homes (since these provide the greatest tax revenue), working people of modest means too often cannot find housing at all.

All of this should give Christians pause. The omnipresent cultural fantasy of the dream house can too easily mask the reality of the nightmare of homelessness or of substandard or precarious housing that affects too many people. People need homes. They don't need fantasies of luxury but the realities of place and nurturance and security. In the words of Habitat for Humanity, the nonprofit organization that builds houses around the world with and for people who could not otherwise afford them, they need "simple, decent shelter."

Many Christian individuals and churches give to and volunteer with organizations like Habitat for Humanity precisely in response to the recognition that one of the most basic ways to share the love of God with our fellow human beings is to offer them shelter. Others are active in their communities in a variety of efforts to increase the availability of affordable housing and of jobs that pay a living wage.

On a more personal level, those of us who are decently housed might think about how we could go about shaping our own attitudes and behavior with respect to the houses in which we live. Here too the fantasy of the dream house is instructive, in that it is so utterly removed from the realities that characterize too many of our houses too much of the time. Clothes and toys lie strewn from one side of the house to the other, there seems to be nowhere to put anything, and we find ourselves wondering whether the whole family is likely to come down with typhoid if the bathroom is left uncleaned for yet another day or week or month. And in the midst of it all, there too often sits someone who is reading a magazine or watching a TV show about the dream house rather than tidying up the house he or she is in.

There has surely always been a gap between the way people keep their houses and the way they would like ideally to keep them. But many of us, I suspect, are demoralized by the task of keeping house in part because we know that our houses, no matter how well kept, will never look like the palaces in the dream house publications. And so we give up, preferring unattainable ideals to less than perfect realities.

An alternative might be humility and gratitude that in a world in which not all are decently housed, we have been given the gift of a home, plus a willingness to aspire to a more modest ideal and to work to achieve it. Instead of nurturing dissatisfaction with the shortcomings of our present home, whatever we may perceive them to be, perhaps we can turn our energies toward receiving as gifts the homes we have and to creating in them enough order and tidiness to promote convenience and peace and hospitality.

HOUSE AND HOME

The physical fabric and setting of the house does matter when it comes to the creation of a home. Urban planners talk about a reciprocal relationship that exists between buildings and their contexts (like neighborhoods and cities), on the one hand, and the character and social relationships of people, on the other hand. Your house, in other words, affects how you live, and how you live affects your house.

This has implications beyond the lives of Christian individuals or households. As one writer notes, "The front door of the home is the side door of the church." What kind of church do our household members and guests encounter when they walk in the front doors of our homes? Do our homes reflect and embody a gospel that takes seriously the needs that all of us, as embodied and social creatures, have for things like beds and clothes and meals and the daily routines that produce them? Does the way we live bear witness to both the necessity and the goodness of things like these? Can we—do we—keep house in ways that respect and embrace our creatureliness and that foster community within and beyond our households?

How are our houses related to the neighborhoods and larger communities of which they are a part? Regrettably, a lot of housing is not helpfully located when it comes to the nuts and bolts of housekeeping. The suburban developments in which increasing numbers of people live are designed to be driven rather than walked and are thus built with long and busy roads between housing and retail establishments like grocery stores and dry cleaners. The result is that you can easily spend half the day driving around doing your marketing and other errands. No wonder you can't get anything done at home—you are never there.

For those who live someplace other than the suburbs, location poses other challenges. If you live in a fifth-floor walk-up, you are going to need to get very organized about shopping so that you are not constantly having to run out for this item or that. If your apartment is on a busy street, you are going to have a lot of dirt coming in through the windows. Whatever your situation, part of making your house into a home will be discerning how the house relates to its particular setting and the opportunities and challenges posed by that location.

Another basic feature of any house is its size. Coffee-table books about "not-so-big houses" notwithstanding, the general rule of thumb about houses seems to be that they are always too small. Even big houses are too small. There is a neighborhood of five- and six-bedroom Queen Anne mansions not far from where I live, and every one of those houses has been added onto. And many of us who live in something more modest than a Queen Anne mansion feel ourselves perpetually pinched for space and longing for more room.

The construction and banking industries are eager to sell us the extra space we crave. The self-storage industry is booming too as more and more people find themselves with more possessions than they have room for. But might it be possible for us to find ways to live in the space we already have? To do so would require that we accept the limits of that space and work creatively and contentedly within them. This is not an easy task when the premise of our culture is that limits are not compatible with either creativity or contentment.

Christian tradition, on the other hand, has been inclined to see limits as a necessary component of human flourishing. The limits imposed by dietary practices like fasting, by marriage, and by modest dress all contribute to helping people live in peaceable and fulfilling relationship to one another and to God. Perhaps the limits of our houses—limits of size or other sorts of limits—can similarly serve to provide us with specific arenas within which to live out our dependence on God and our interdependence on one another.

Giving attention to beauty is part of the work involved in making a house a home. While it can be tempting to imagine that interior decoration is a sub-Christian concern, if there is one thing the authors of scripture are at pains to tell us about the dwelling places that God has made for his people and has instructed his people to make for him, it is that they are beautiful. The Garden of Eden was beautiful, the tabernacle was beautiful, the temple was beautiful, the city of Jerusalem is beautiful, and the New Jerusalem will be the most beautiful of all, with streets paved with gold and walls set with jewels.

Not all budgets will allow for gold and jewels, or even decorator fabrics. And of course there is the question whether this is necessarily the best way for a Christian to spend his or her money. Is a luxuriously beautiful home like the perfume that Mary of Magdala poured over Jesus' head—costly, and worth every penny? Or is it a misuse of money that would have been better given to the poor? The answer is probably not the same in every case. For the many people who cannot possibly afford expensive décor, the point is moot. To those who, like me, fall into this latter category, I have one word of advice: paint.

I was reminded of the power of paint one day when my son was four and we had been away from home visiting relatives for rather too long. As he was getting ready to go to sleep, he looked around the room and said, "Why are all the walls white?" "Well," I said, "I suppose someone thought that would look nice." "But our walls at home are colored," he said. "They're red and blue and green and purple and silver and brown. . . ."

Later that evening I wrote to a friend, "Here we have this pathetic little shoebox of a house, whose walls we have painted a jumble of unlikely colors out of sheer desperation, but it appears that to Mark, it is a lovely little jewel box of a home, and he misses it when we are away." Do I wish I had a house that was more naturally beautiful? Yes, I do. But through the eyes of a child, the house we have is beautiful. We've done what we can with what we have, and it is good enough. It is a home.

HOUSEHOLD GOODS

The term "household goods" is commonly used to refer to the objects that help us live conveniently and comfortably in our homes—beds, desks, tables, chairs, lamps, curtains. But there is another sense in which we can use the term, in reference to decisions we make about how to live in the house itself. Where will we eat? Where will we sleep? Will we dedicate particular spaces to particular uses, or will we do many things in one place? If we share our household with others, will we share the physical dwelling space by using it in common or by partitioning it?

Household members do not start from scratch as they decide how to live in their homes. Architects design dwellings with particular patterns of use in mind. You can tell that no one is expected actually to use the living room and dining room of a new house, because these spaces are small and placed at the front of the home, far from the primary entrance, which is the one from the garage. The main living space in most new houses is the "great room," a combined kitchen and family room that spans the back of the structure, with a microwave oven at one end and a blank wall intended to accommodate an enormous entertainment center at the other end.

The assumption behind such an arrangement is that home is first and foremost a docking station for the consumption of electronic entertainment. The natural tendency of anyone living in such a house is not going to be to cook a meal and eat it at a nicely set table with whoever else lives in the house. The tendency is going to be to microwave a frozen burrito and eat it in front of the television. It is simply easier to go with the grain of the house than to go against it.

Easier, but not obligatory. No one has to own a widescreen television, after all. If we furnish our homes with cooking and eating and conversation and sleeping in mind, we will be more likely to live in them in ways that foster nourishment and refreshment and engagement with the routines that sustain the bodies and souls of individuals and of communities. And if we get rid of our televisions (or at least make them small and tuck them into a corner), we will at the same time eliminate one of the most demoralizing and distasteful chores associated with housekeeping, that of picking up after people who spend their days sitting around watching TV.

Where personal space is concerned, the trend in our culture has long been toward increasing privacy. People of our grandparents' generation shared their beds with their siblings when they were children. People of our parents' generation probably shared a room with a brother or a sister. Many of us grew up with our own rooms, and many of today's children are growing up with their own bathrooms—to the dismay of the designers of college dormitories, who find themselves trying to house a generation of young people who have never shared a bathroom and aren't about to start now.

Will we order our homes in accordance with this trend toward ever-increasing isolation even within the confines of our homes? Or will we set up our homes in ways that encourage household members actually to live in community with one another? I have a friend who has four sons, and when the children were small, the family lived in a large house in which each of the boys could have had his own room. Instead, my friend put two pairs of bunk beds in one room and called it the bedroom and put the toys in another room and called it the playroom. Her sons' experiences of home and family were probably as deeply affected by this ordering of the geography of their house as they were by anything else.

There are, on the other hand, households whose members have no choice but to share their space. I think of friends who have three or four children and live in two-bedroom homes in which the baby's crib is in the hall. I think of my own two-bedroom home, which even though it shelters only three people still seems mighty cramped. Every room has multiple purposes; we are all within sight of one another most of the time. Is the house "too small"? Well, yes, it is. And yet there is value in having to cultivate intentionally the art of sharing what space we have as an aspect of living peaceably with one another.

As good as sharing space may be, there is a role for privacy as well. Privacy is a highly socially constructed category, with one end of the spectrum represented by the American cultural ideal of near-complete isolation (witness the current fashion in high-end homes for separate his-and-hers bathrooms in the master suite). But even Jesus, who lived in community with his twelve disciples and was incarnate for the sake of all humanity, felt from time to time a need for time and space apart from others. And most people likewise feel some desire for a place apart, a quiet space that is theirs alone, that no one else uses and no one else messes up and that can be a nurturing and restorative place for that individual.

Such a place is particularly important for any person who devotes a lot of energy to keeping house for others. The homemaker needs a home too. This is so even for someone who loves to keep house and is willing and able to give it the time it takes to do it well. It is all the more true for the person who does not especially enjoy housekeeping or who is doing it under trying circumstances (such as while simultaneously looking after preschool children). If the house is large, perhaps this place can be a separate office or a sewing room. If it is small, it might be just a special chair or private desk. Whatever particular form it takes, this can be a place that offers restoration and renewal in the midst of the many demands of family and of work, whether at home or elsewhere.

Houses need furniture if they are to function as homes, as places that are ready to receive members of the household or their guests in a hospitable manner. Various Christian authors have suggested that the preparation of a "Christ room," a place simply furnished so as to be able to receive a guest, can be a powerful symbol of the keeping of a Christian home. And the furnishing of the entire house for the use of household members is arguably at least as foundational. People need beds in which to sleep; they need a table at which to eat, chairs in which to sit, light by which to read or study, carpets and curtains for comfort and for beauty.

Not all of these furnishings have to be equally special. Indeed, the house is likely to be more beautiful if they are not. One person I know makes the point this way: "Beware too many masterpieces." He can, he says, always tell the good cooks from the bad cooks when he goes to the supermarket. The bad cooks' shopping carts are filled with shrimp and lobster and filet mignon. The good cooks choose a bag, he says, of rice and one fat truffle. Furnishing a beautiful home works the same way: it requires only a handful of beautiful objects.

I think this person's point is valid even for those of us whose budgets run more to mushrooms and tuna than to truffles and lobster. The way to a beautiful home is not to buy, or aspire to buy, lots of expensively beautiful things. Often all it takes to give beauty to a home is that it not be overfilled with too many things of any kind and then that there be just a few objects of special beauty or meaning. Everything else can come from a garage sale, and it will still be a place that is not just comfortable but lovely.

In my house there are two rocking chairs made by a North Carolina country chairmaker and a small cupboard made by a Philadelphia cabinetmaker. Practically everything else in the house is forgettable. The result is that everyone who enters the house is drawn to the beautiful chairs and cupboard, and even though they use the other furniture, they don't notice it. It is rather like hospitality itself—part warmly inviting and part unobtrusive and self-effacing.

A PLACE FOR EVERYTHING?

Picking up a house requires that there be places to put things—and then that we put them there. Dirty clothes go in the hamper, dirty dishes in the sink, toys in the cupboard, books on the shelf, newspapers in the recycling bin. It sounds so easy, and it would be, if not for one of the great menaces of modern life: clutter.

It is all too easy to think of clutter as one of the inevitabilities of life when in fact it is a product of our culture. We live in a society in which virtually everyone has more belongings than he or she can comfortably find room for. The average family is smaller than ever, the average new house is bigger than ever, and one of the growth industries in affluent areas characterized by big new houses is that of professional organizers who specialize in cleaning out oversized, overstuffed garages.

But clutter is not just a problem for people who have more money than "we" do, whoever "we" are. It doesn't seem to matter how much money or space anyone has; they spend their money and fill up their space, and then they spend more and fill more, to the point that they can't figure out how to get out from under the huge mounds of stuff they have accumulated. It is so easy to acquire ever more possessions, and the temptation is so great to imagine that somehow we will find room for them, that over and over again we succumb, even when experience ought to tell us otherwise.

Just how problematic this is is suggested by comments like those of the host of the cable television show *Clean House,* which features professional cleaners tidying up other people's messes. Asked by an interviewer what advice she would give to someone whose house is in serious need of help, the host replied, "You know what they say: after you binge, go home and purge. That's as simple as I can make it— go home and purge."

It is a fascinating, disturbing image, made all the more so by the casual assumption that what it describes is normal and unremarkable. This television personality assumes that people necessarily deal with our culture's overwhelming abundance of food by alternately gorging themselves on it and vomiting it up. And she concludes that they must do the same thing with the culture's overwhelming abundance of consumer goods: first they binge and then they purge.

As Christians, we are called to respond differently to abundance. Many things in life, whether food or household objects, are truly good. They are to be treated with appreciation and respect, and sometimes this means saying no to too much. This does not necessarily mean being "less materialistic." In a way, it means being more materialistic. It means taking material things seriously enough to be willing to get rid of them or to decline to acquire them in the first place.

In a society in which you are what you have, this is not as straightforward as it might seem. One upscale lifestyle magazine routinely features articles about how to avoid throwing away things like old food cans (wash them out and use them to hold plastic utensils at your next casual party) and old orange rinds (put them in the freezer and bring them out as serving dishes for ice cream at that same party).

Suggestions like these may sound frugal, but they are not. They are acquisitiveness disguised as frugality. They make sense only on the assumption that people have unlimited storage space (which is not true of anyone, regardless of the size of his or her house) or that they have unlimited time and enthusiasm for putting things into storage and taking them out again (which is unlikely to be true of anyone whose life also includes things like work or family or church).

The reality is that for all of us, whether we live in a cottage or a castle, whether we shop garage sales or at the mall, space and time are limited. Having a tidy and pleasant house requires that we recognize those limits and live within them. Are we saving or acquiring things because we actually need them and will use them? Or are we saving or acquiring things simply because we like to shop and we like to treasure things up?

It can be simple wisdom to allow available space—the size of a closet, a cupboard, a shelf—to limit the number of things that we save or acquire for any purpose. The seventeenth-century diarist Samuel Pepys is supposed to have kept his library in two cupboards called bookpresses. Once the bookpresses were full, he bought a new book only if at the same time he got rid of a book he already had so that his library never exceeded the capacity of the bookpresses.

Pepys was no doubt encouraged to limit the size of his library by the fact that in the seventeenth century, books deteriorated rapidly if kept anywhere but a bookpress. People today are tempted to keep limitless volumes of stuff, at least in part because much of it comes with guarantees that it will last more or less forever (think, for example, of the acid-free supplies sold for making scrapbooks). On the heels of these guarantees comes a temptation to ascribe a kind of eternality and infinitude both to ourselves and to our possessions. But only God is without limits. People are finite and do well to live in ways that reflect that reality.

Perhaps the hardest things to dispose of, or to decline to acquire in the first place, are things you like and would certainly use if you kept them but that you do not have room for. One fall I was scavenging around used bookstores in search of paperback books to send to a friend who lives abroad with her four small children. As I sorted through the books at home, it occurred to me that I didn't own any other copies of most of these books, and my own son was approaching an age when he might be ready for many of them. Should I keep them? But where would I put them? I took a deep breath, boxed up the books, and sent them off to Uganda.

The fact is, there are a lot of lovely and useful things in this world, and our houses and our lives simply do not have room for most of them. We have to learn to say no, and to say no not just to things we don't need or want but also to things we might very well enjoy. I find myself saying this nearly every day to my son, who has heard loud and clear the cultural message about the delights of shopping. But I have to say it to myself as well. No, I cannot have more clothes, more pots and pans, more books, more things. The house is full. There is no room. Or rather, there is a limited amount of room, and it is already spoken for.

When there are limits to the numbers of things and the kinds of things there are in a house, the house can become a place that moves back and forth comfortably from being messy to being tidy. Houses inevitably become messy because people live there, and they are busy with all manner of things. But if there are places to put things and it is simple and convenient to put them there, then picking up the house becomes a kind of active meditation, like putting a favorite puzzle together and seeing the familiar picture—the tidy house—appear anew.

IS CLEANLINESS NEXT
TO GODLINESS?

Cleaning is one task among many in the work of keeping a house, and yet there can be a tendency to see cleanliness as the sole benchmark of competence in housekeeping. "So-and-so is a good housekeeper" is often just another way of saying "So-and-so's house is clean." Is this really fair? Is the only good housekeeper one of whom it can truly be said, "You could eat off her floor!"? Who wants to eat off a floor, anyway? What is the point, precisely, of having a clean house? Is there virtue in spotlessness? Is dirt a sign of poor character? And just how clean is clean?

It is true that Christian scripture uses cleanliness as a metaphor for purity and acceptability to God and soiling as a metaphor for disobedience and sin. These metaphors tended to collapse into near-identification in American culture around the end of the nineteenth century and the beginning of the twentieth, with the rise of the germ theory of disease and the origins of modern chemical detergents and disinfectants.

The new ability to trace disease directly to bacteria and to prevent the spread of disease by washing away bacteria-laden dirt gave rise to such innovations in Christian faith and practice as the individual communion cup. Yes, church leaders acknowledged, Christians had up to now always used a common cup, tracing that usage to Jesus' example at the Last Supper and finding in the common cup a powerful symbol of Christian unity. But, they argued, the fact that Jesus shared a cup with his friends does not imply that all Christians should share a cup with whatever (potentially dirty) strangers might enter their churches. Christians today should therefore reject the germy common cup in favor of sanitary individual ones.

Not everyone accepted this line of reasoning, which is why not all church bodies converted to the use of individual communion cups. But it does show the complex interplay between cultural and theological forces when it comes to so seemingly mundane a consideration as how clean is clean and what kind of cleanliness is expected to characterize a Christian individual or group.

Social and scientific forces come into play as well. "Jesus does not live in dirt," an elderly black lady of my acquaintance declared to me one day. I suspect that this lady's floors are clean enough to eat off of. I suspect further that in her life she has encountered many closed doors, but one open door has been the opportunity to keep a clean house, with all the potential excellence and beauty that that involves.

The fact is, standards of cleanliness vary. The meaning of cleanliness varies too. I have two friends whom I'll call Ann and Joan. Ann's mother kept a spotless house, mostly (Ann has come to believe) as one means among many of exerting iron-fisted control over everyone in her household. Joan's mother kept a chaotically messy house, mostly (Joan has come to believe) because she just didn't care about the comfort or convenience of anyone else in the household.

One day Ann confided to Joan that she loved to visit Joan's mother's house. "The mess!" Ann said. "I just sit there in the midst of it all and think, 'This woman just doesn't care!' It is so freeing!" It had never occurred to Joan that anyone could experience her mother's messiness this way. But in fact, if there was a problem with Joan's mother's housekeeping, it was not (or at least mostly not) that the house was "too messy." It was that the effect of the messiness on the rest of the household was inhospitable.

And the same was true of Ann's mother's housekeeping. That house was clean, and the effect of the cleanliness was to make the other members of the household feel unwelcome in their own home. I have another friend whose own tendency is to keep a very tidy home. She finds herself consciously ratcheting back her expectations and practices from time to time, lest her daughters grow up to say of their childhoods, "We cleaned up a lot."

How clean any individual or household chooses to keep a house will depend on many things. How clean does the house have to be to feel comfortable to you or to others in the household? How much time do you have to devote to cleaning? If there are other members of the household, would you prefer that everyone share in the cleaning chores or that some of you vacate the house every so often so that the others can clean in happy peace? And how clean is really reasonable or desirable, given the particulars of your circumstances?

Take floors, for example. My first husband was Korean. We took off our shoes in the house. We hardly ever cleaned the floors because there was never any dirt on them. My second husband uses a wheelchair. It is just not practical to require a wheelchair user to wipe his wheels when he comes in the door. Add to that a small boy who exerts a magnetic attraction to dirt, two dogs, and a yard that has as many bare patches as grassy bits. Now I wear my shoes in the house, to keep my socks clean, and every so often my son (who despite his personal scruffiness likes to clean) gets down on his hands and knees and scrubs bits of the floor with a washcloth.

Any two or more people who form a household are likely to find themselves in the midst of negotiations about how clean the house should be and how it should get that way. Most of us discover how strong our preferences are precisely as we discover that our spouses or housemates have different preferences. The challenges of living in community come down, more often than not, to intensely practical matters like which sponge gets used for what.

One way to handle these differences is to have the person who cares the most about how something is cleaned be the one to clean it. Another way is for other members of the household to adopt the standards of the person who cares more about it—not because that person is the boss but simply as a gift to him or her. Many of us feel more strongly about cleaning than we like to admit, and so doing something somebody else's way can be a significant step toward that other person.

Perhaps the biggest cleaning challenges are the spaces that don't get used much—both big ones (like attics, basements, and garages) and small ones (like closets and drawers). Cleaning these spaces is often very different from cleaning the rest of the house. These spaces are not used every day, and they are often not used for any particular purpose. They turn into catchall spaces; we put things in them in order to delay or avoid making decisions about whether these are things we really need and have room for.

Dealing with these spaces presents an opportunity to tell the truth about what we have, what we need, and what we truly have room for. I have a friend who has boxes of books in his attic, all carefully indexed and cross-referenced so he can find what he wants when he wants it. But, he ruefully admits, when he actually needs one of those books, it always seems easier just to go to the bookstore and buy a new copy. What would happen if he were to take all his boxes of books to the used bookstore? At the very least, he would have the opportunity to discover what it is like to have an attic that is empty rather than full.

Empty space, even a little bit of it, is good to have. It is good on a practical level, in that if the attic or the closets are not full of things that are never used, it will be easier to get to the things that do get used. But empty space is good on a psychic and symbolic level as well. A primary objective of keeping house is to make room—room for connecting and reconnecting with other people and with the rhythms of individual and common life: meals, rest, work, play. As we made decisions about what to put in our houses and what to take out of them, we have the opportunity to make room in those houses for ourselves, for our fellow household members, and for guests.

Clothes to Wear

I n Else Minarik's classic children's story *Little Bear,* the title character wants to play outside but finds that he is cold. "Mother Bear," he says, "I need something to put on." Mother Bear obliges, producing first a hat, then a coat, then snowpants. Little Bear is still not satisfied, and finally Mother Bear takes away the hat, the coat, and the snowpants, revealing the fur coat that Little Bear has on underneath. Little Bear goes out to play, and he is not cold. The story concludes with a metaphorical wink of the eye: "Now what do you think of that?"

Small children find this story entertaining because they know full well that animals do not need to get dressed because they are not naked. People, on the other hand, do have to get dressed. What they wear depends on a lot of different things—how old they are, in what culture or climate they live, what they do for work, how wealthy or poor they are. But everybody has to get dressed, because without clothes, people are naked.

The themes of clothing and nakedness run through Christian scripture virtually from its first page to its last. When Adam and Eve disobey God by eating from the fruit of the tree that God had forbidden them to touch, Adam is afraid and hides from God because, he says, "I was naked." Whether nakedness is really the first problem that Adam and Eve are aware of in the wake of their sin or whether it is simply the first problem that they are willing to admit to, nakedness serves throughout the rest of the Bible as a metaphor for and a symptom of human sinfulness and need.

Clothing, for its part, serves as a symbol of care and protection, beginning with God's provision of clothing for Adam and Eve in the wake of their sin: "The Lord God made for Adam and for his wife garments of skins, and clothed them" (Genesis 3:21). The people of Israel are clothed by God during their sojourn in the wilderness and are enjoined similarly to clothe the stranger in their midst (Deuteronomy 10:18). Isaiah envisions Israel's eventual redemption in terms of clothing: "Awake, awake, put on your strength, O Zion, put on your beautiful garments, O Jerusalem, the holy city" (52:1).

All good things can be misused or abused, and clothing is no exception. Joseph is the favored son of his father, Jacob, and as a sign of that favor, Jacob gives him a special piece of clothing, a "coat of many colors" (as the King James Version translates) or a "long robe with sleeves" (per the Revised Standard Version). Joseph's brothers, who resent his status as the favorite, strip him of his robe, throw him into a pit, and sell him into slavery. Then they dip his robe in goat's blood and show it to their father, who concludes that Joseph has been killed by wild animals.

In this story, there is nothing redemptive about clothing. Clothing is used to demonstrate favoritism; it kindles strife, becomes a means of deceit, and ends as the object of a gesture of grief: "Then Jacob rent his garments, and put sackcloth upon his loins, and mourned for his son many days" (Genesis 37:34). Many people after Jacob mourn their losses similarly: Job rends his garments upon hearing of the deaths of his children (Job 1:20); King Hezekiah does likewise upon hearing of the defeat of his troops (Isaiah 37:1), as do various of the prophets as they reflect on the infidelities and sins of Israel.

The life and ministry of Christ are similarly characterized by metaphors and images of clothing and unclothing, from the swaddling clothes in which Jesus is wrapped at his birth (Luke 2:7) to the shroud in which he is wrapped at his death (Mark 15:46). When a woman touches Jesus' garment, she is healed (Matthew 9:20–22). When Jesus is transfigured, his garments become as white as light (Matthew 17:2). At the Last Supper, Jesus lays aside his garments to wash the disciples' feet and puts them back on afterward to teach (John 13:3–12). At his crucifixion Jesus is again unclothed, and soldiers divide and cast lots for his garments (Mark 15:24). At his resurrection Jesus leaves his graveclothes in the grave (John 20:5–7), and his resurrection is announced by angels who are themselves clothed in "dazzling apparel" (Luke 24:4).

Some of the New Testament's most powerful images of redemption are images of nakedness and clothing. Paul, writing to the Corinthian church, says, "For we know that if the earthly tent we live in is destroyed, we have a building from God, a house not made with hands, eternal in the heavens. Here indeed we groan, and long to put on our heavenly dwelling, so that by putting it on we may not be found naked. For while we are still in this tent, we sigh with anxiety; not that we would be unclothed, but that we would be further clothed, so that what is mortal may be swallowed up by life" (2 Corinthians 5:1–4).

Nakedness, for Paul, is a symbol or a symptom of human frailty and neediness, and clothing is a kind of temporary and anticipatory remedy. Our bodies clothe us during our earthly pilgrimage, and we clothe our bodies during that pilgrimage. Redemption consists not in being restored to some primal, unashamed nakedness but in being finally fully clothed, with bodies that are truly alive and in clothing that is truly glorious.

CLOTHING AND IDENTITY

Our bodies are the vehicles through which we encounter and experience the world and through which others encounter and experience us. We are not reducible to our bodies, but neither do we live or move or have our being in any way other than in and through the bodies we have. Insofar as our bodies are healthy and capable and attractive, this may be a source of pleasure to ourselves and to others. When our bodies fail us in some way—when we experience ill health or disability or a simple lack of some desirable ability or beauty— we experience this as a loss or as a source of suffering.

Clothing serves as a kind of extension of the body, in that we encounter and experience the world at least in part through the clothes we wear. This is true, to begin with, in a very straightforward physical sense. The Swedes, who inhabit a part of the world not known for its hospitable climate, have a saying: "There is no bad weather, only bad clothes." Given proper clothing, even a landscape characterized by snow or ice or rain or cold can be not only inhabitable but also beautiful. Lacking proper clothing, we may struggle just to survive.

Clothing helps chart our paths through our social worlds as well. The clothes we wear signal who we are. John the Baptist wore clothing made of camel hair and a belt made of leather because he was a prophet, and that is what prophets wear. The prophet Elijah had dressed the same way, in a garment of haircloth and with a girdle of leather (1 Kings 1:8). So characteristic is this dress that a prophet who wishes to conceal his identity has only to leave his camel's hair clothing in his closet; Zechariah refers to such shamefaced prophets in his own ministry (13:4).

Not many people are wearing camel's hair these days, at least not in forms that signal prophetic status. But people do rely on clothing as a means of self-expression and self-identification. Most of us exercise considerable power over what we wear. The very poor have to take what they are given, but most other people have a broad range of choices, within the limits imposed by their bodies and their budgets. Often we hold those choices dear, resisting things like dress codes and uniforms that shift the focus from individuality to membership in a group and regarding as slightly eccentric those who minimize their own options in clothing, like the university professor I once knew who wore a black suit every single day of the year, no matter the weather or the agenda.

Clothing choices can be aspirational as well as expressive. We may buy clothes based not on who we are but on who we wish we were. People who wish they were thinner may buy clothes that will fit them, they hope, after they lose a few pounds. People who wish they could afford designer clothing buy designer knock-offs. Personal finance columnists relate stories of wealthy women who can well afford real designer clothing and who buy it all in black, the better to disguise new purchases from the disapproving eyes of their husbands, from whom, apparently, they wish they were freer.

Even just trying to dress as who we are is complicated by the enormous range of choices available in clothing. A psychologist who writes about the effects of choice on consumer behavior tells a story about his experience of going to a well-known chain store to buy a pair of jeans and being confronted with a choice of over fifty different styles. He entered the store with the intention of purchasing a pair of jeans identical to the ones he was wearing, but before long he had no idea what to choose, so overwhelmed was he by the number of options and by the seeming importance of choosing just the right one.

Perhaps it is our lack of confidence in our ability to choose the right clothes that leads so many of us to purchase and to own far more clothing than we actually wear. I know a few people with large wardrobes who seem to wear something different every day and look good in it all. I know more people who poke through closets overflowing with wrinkled, mismatched clothing, looking for something, anything, to wear. Somehow, we just aren't the people we thought we were when we bought those things; none of them seems right.

When we are responsible for dressing other people, the stakes go up: their clothing says something about both them and us. What sort of people are we to allow our family members to go out dressed like that? I have a friend who confessed to replacing her husband's holey socks not because he cared about the holes but because she worried that his socks would reflect badly on her. I know of another woman who, when her preschool-age daughter began to insist on constructing her own outfits, would pin a note to the back of her clothes: "I dressed myself today." She was willing, in other words, for her daughter to be seen in public wearing a red plaid kilt with a striped T-shirt and pink plastic sandals, but only if no one blamed her for it.

It seems that many of us would like, if only in a secret corner of ourselves, to be like the virtuous woman in Proverbs 31 of whom we read that "all her household is clothed in scarlet." Their clothes are warm, in other words, and beautiful and substantive, and—best of all—they reflect well on the person who provided those clothes. Most people nowadays provide their households with clothing by buying it rather than by making it, but we are as sensitive as people have ever been to what clothes are the right clothes. We want our households to be clothed, if not in scarlet, then in whatever sort of clothing signals that they are well dressed.

Unsurprisingly, people don't always agree as to what amounts to dressing well. Like the preschooler who likes plaid with stripes, our household members may have strong ideas about what they like and who they are that are not necessarily the same as ours. Unless the only person you are dressing is yourself, you won't always be able to have it your way. The challenge will be to send people out the door in the morning wearing clothes that reflect an appropriate mix of who we want them to be and believe that they are and who they believe themselves to be and want to be.

It is not always easy to discern when to insist, when to negotiate, and when to yield without comment. Friends with daughters tell me of the complexities of negotiating modest clothing in a society in which the assumption is that female bodies are to be displayed rather than veiled. My son informed me when he was four that while girls want to look pretty, boys want to look cool. Since then there have been many days when his ideas of cool and my ideas of appropriate have not been the same.

Even spouses are not always willing to wear what we think best. My first husband had opinions about sweaters: they had to be wool, and they had to come all the way up to his neck. I expended a lot of energy trying to get him to wear the cotton V-neck sweaters that were then fashionable before I finally realized that what he wore was up to him, not me.

My identity did not include his clothes, and the more room we each had to wear what made us feel ready to encounter the world, the happier we both were.

TO EVERYTHING ITS SEASON

The clothes we wear mediate the seasonality of our lives and our relationships in ways that are gradually disappearing in other spheres of life. Spring cleaning is a relic of a bygone age when there were no vacuum cleaners and carpets could only be cleaned by being untacked, hung on clotheslines, and swatted with carpet-beaters. Spring chickens are gone completely, replaced by factory-raised poultry that know no seasons. But spring clothes, Easter outfits, short-sleeved tops dug out of drawers and put on at the first breath of warm weather—these are still with us.

Clothing is seasonal in the obvious sense of corresponding to the seasons of the year. If we live in a temperate climate, we will wear lightweight clothing in the summer, sweaters in the fall, coats and boots in the winter, and navy blue with polka dots in the spring (but of course no white shoes before Memorial Day). Well, maybe not. The physical requirements of seasonality are overlaid, in other words, with cultural ideas of what is appropriate to any given season. Who decided that red and green are the colors of Christmas? I don't know, but I do have a friend who has a red-and-green-plaid sport jacket that he hauls out every year at Christmastime.

Wearing, and providing others with, clothes appropriate to the season of the year is a way of living in harmony with the God-given character of our surroundings. We all know small children who resist wearing a jacket when it is cold out and have to be reminded that in the winter, we dress for winter. But adults can find this a challenge too. I read a newspaper article once about a fashion trend that involved adult women wearing short, thin dresses in the middle of the northern winter. I don't remember how these women were said to have avoided frostbite, although presumably they didn't spend much time outside in these outfits.

Fashion statements like these may seem trivial—why should it matter what people wear in the cold as long as they're happy in it? But if a person's choice of clothing seems to reveal complete disengagement from the climate in which she lives, what does this suggest about that person's degree of connection in other aspects of her life? The more our clothing relates us directly and comfortably to the specific times and places in which we live, the more likely it seems that we will be able to relate directly and hospitably to the other persons whose lives touch ours.

Seasonality is about more than weather. Our own lives have seasons to them: childhood and adulthood, singleness and marriage, before children and after children, work and retirement. Many traditional societies still demarcate sharply these seasons of life and often signal that demarcation by the kinds of clothes that people wear. Young children are dressed differently from adolescents; married women dress differently from single women; older people dress differently from younger people.

People who live in the modern West are sometimes unaware of any customs relating their mode of dress to their time of life and sometimes actively resist such customs as remain. Thus we see, for example, the blurring of distinctions between children's and adult fashions and the increasing tendency of parents and children to dress in ways that are equally mature or equally childish. And yet there are still ways in which our clothing does in fact mirror and participate in our seasons of life.

Maternity clothes are perhaps the most obvious example of such clothing. Some women eagerly anticipate the time when their changing bodies will demand maternity clothes and their pregnancies will become obvious and public. Other women are more reluctant to don maternity clothes, wishing, perhaps, that their pregnancies did not have to be quite so public. Most women I know have become heartily sick of their maternity clothes by the time they finally give birth and gladly pack them away after their babies are born—and yet when they come across those clothes in some later bout of closet cleaning, they find them laden with memories, taking them back to the days when children now well along in life were still eagerly awaited strangers.

Clothes themselves have their seasons, from new to not-so-new to old to raggedy. Some people are very methodical about keeping track of where on this continuum a piece of clothing lies. My maternal grandfather was an engineer whose wardrobe included dozens of identical white dress shirts, each with a number neatly inked onto the label. A higher number meant a newer shirt; he reserved the half-dozen newest shirts for formal occasions, the next dozen for work, and the dozen below that for wear around the house or in his workshop. Shirts with really low numbers got torn up and used as cleaning rags by my grandmother.

Utterly dissimilar to my grandfather's shirt-numbering system is the currently fashionable practice of buying clothes that are "distressed"; that is, that come already worn out, complete with holes and faded fabric. These are clothes for people who don't want to wait, who can't be bothered to wear a pair of jeans for the years that it takes to get them to that comfortably worn stage. They are clothes for people who want new clothes upon which machines have inflicted the likeness of age. This practice turns seasonality on its head, asking for autumn while actively rejecting spring.

And at the same time as some people are shopping for clothes that look old but aren't, others are busy trying to make their bodies look young when they aren't. Owners of high-end clothing stores find that the wealthy women who are their customers now pour enormous amounts of energy into stringent exercise regimens and as a result are getting thinner and thinner. Boutiques that used to do most of their business in size 8's now do most of their volume in 6's and 4's. The owner of one such shop says, "Sometimes women come in and say, 'Oh, you can't fit me,' and I say, 'You've made yourself into a child, and this is not a store for children.'"

There is a time for everything. The way we treat both our bodies and our clothes can reflect our willingness—or unwillingness—to live in the moment, at the particular time and in the particular circumstances in which we find ourselves. The seasons of our lives come and go. We do not have to hurry them along, for the future will be here soon enough. Neither do we need desperately to try to make time stand still, as if that were possible. God is lord of time; if he gloriously clothes the lilies of the field that bloom one day and are gone the next, will he not also clothe and care for us?

SPECIAL CLOTHES
FOR SPECIAL DAYS

Seasons are punctuated by special days and times. This is so in civil calendars: what would summer be without the Fourth of July, fall without Thanksgiving, winter without New Year's Day, spring without Memorial Day? Perhaps more significant for Christians are the special days of the Christian year: Christmas, Epiphany, Good Friday, Palm Sunday, Easter, Pentecost. And the lives of each of us as individuals include special days—birthdays, anniversaries, days of rejoicing, and days of mourning.

We mark our special days with special clothes. We see this especially in central life-cycle events: birth, marriage, death. We choose a special outfit for a new baby to wear home from the hospital; we take new clothes as a gift to an adopted child when we first meet him or her. We dress our children and ourselves in special clothes for baptism. We wear celebratory clothes to our own weddings and to the weddings of others. We wear somber clothes when we attend a funeral or when someone we know or love has died.

When we put on special clothes, we are saying something to ourselves and to others about who we are and what this occasion is about. There are a couple of ways of doing this, one that has the character of a myth and one that has the character of a parable. A myth is a big story that gives meaning to other, little stories. A parable is a little story that forms a window into a bigger story. The Germanic myths that Wagner set to music expressed a certain (pagan) understanding of life, the universe, and everything else. The parables Jesus told about a woman sweeping her house and men sowing seeds offered his listeners a glimpse of the kingdom of God.

The most mythic of contemporary American rituals is the wedding, and its central garment is the wedding dress. As scholars of popular culture point out, the twin idols of American culture are consumerism and romance, and lavish weddings offer a perfect opportunity to worship at both of these altars at once. The cake, the limo, and above all the dress constitute an opportunity to pretend to be someone we are not in a story that we wish were true. Thus more and more couples every year choose to marry at Disneyland, and the vast majority of those who do so opt for the "Princess" package, in which the bride makes her entrance in Cinderella's magical coach.

But dressing up does not have to amount to a mythic vacation from reality. Dressing up can be a way of expressing one's awareness that this particular event is not all there is, that there is a bigger story that each of us is a part of and that gives shape and meaning and coherence to the individual moments of our individual lives. The Episcopal theologian Robert Farrar Capon offers a wonderful argument in favor of black-tie dinner parties, namely, that heaven is all about feasting and that it is therefore an act of Christian faithfulness occasionally to put on tuxedos and formal gowns and anticipate the heavenly banquet.

I don't own a formal gown, and neither do most of the people I know. If we were to try to put on a dinner party like the ones Capon describes, I suspect this would amount more to mythic masquerade than to parabolic expectation. But I do get dressed up, on some occasions more than others, and as I do so, I express the truth that my life is about more than me. Dressy clothes tend to be conservative in style (especially for men, whose formal clothing may change little from one generation to the next), and in this way and others they embody the ties that bind people together over time. Our lives are connected with those of others, past, present, and future, and the wearing of special clothes on special days is one way of expressing that connectedness.

Sometimes special clothes and special days are related to the work we do. Nursing school students used to have ceremonies in which they received their nurses' caps. Medical school students still have ceremonies in which they receive their white coats. As a college teacher, one of my jobs is to put on my academic robes and walk in procession with my faculty colleagues on commencement day. All of these types of clothing signify membership in professions that are bigger than any individual person and his or her job.

In the church, special clothes are associated with membership in the clergy or in religious orders. In a Catholic understanding, a priest is fundamentally different from a layperson, and his clerical collar and vestments serve to signal that difference. Protestants understand the clergy as different in function but not in being from the laity. For that reason many Protestants have preferred that their clergy dress not as priests (in cope and alb) but as teachers (in the gown of the university professor).

Other special clothes and days are related simply to membership in the human community. We have all been bereaved, some of us perhaps earlier in life or more tragically than others, but all of us at some time or in some way. The wearing of mourning—special clothes, usually black—may have been practiced in the past in ways that were overly formal or rigid and that unnecessarily separated mourners from the rest of the community. But wearing mourning can be a way of expressing both the reality of one's own loss ("My loved one died, and this changes everything, including what I wear") and its social implications ("Others have had their losses; now I join them on the mourning bench").

And of course joyful days have their special clothes too. Just because modern America is in the grip of wedding mania does not mean that a wedding is not an occasion for a special party and a special dress. The problem with so many weddings is not that they are celebratory; it is that they are celebratory in a way and on a scale that is completely disconnected from the lives of the people involved (as is suggested by their cost, which in many cases exceeds what most of us will ever spend on anything other than a house or a college education).

Why not, instead, have a wedding and a wedding dress that properly belong to you and not to Cinderella? The first time I was married, I wore a long white dress that had been made for my great-grandmother by her stepmother. My own mother had worn it in her turn, as had one of my aunts. The second time I was married, I decided to wear pink, thinking this more suitable for a widow than white. After much shopping, I found a pink suit that needed just a little alteration to fit perfectly. Then, four days before the wedding, there was a medical emergency in my fiancé's family. We decided to be married immediately so that we could join his family halfway across the country. But the pink suit hadn't been altered yet. There was, however, a pair of old pink cotton slacks hanging in my closet, all pressed and ready to wear. I was married four hours later, wearing the pink pants.

I look back on those two weddings with equal satisfaction. The first wedding took place in the midst of family members who had traveled from far and wide to be there; the second, in the presence of several dozen friends who had dropped everything to be at the church that evening. To the first wedding I wore a dress that had been worn by generations of brides before me; to the second, an outfit that wasn't anything special, perhaps, but that was there when I needed it. Both weddings were occasions on which the sometimes hidden connections between my own life and the lives of others and the Christian story of which we are all a part came into view. One day there will be a wedding supper that is the supper of the Lamb, and we all will put on our wedding garments and sit down to feast together.

MAKING THINGS

I have a friend whose husband-to-be gave her a sewing machine as a wedding present. "I'll never be rich," he said, "so you'd better learn to use this." Happily, she was willing to forgive him for this rather unromantic bit of practicality. She also never learned to use the sewing machine. She is, as it turns out, just as practical as he, and it didn't take her long to figure out that it is more expensive to make clothing than it is to buy it.

The making of clothing is in fact one of the aspects of preindustrial housewifery that in the industrialized world has moved from the realm of the home to the realm of the factory. People do still sew at home, and knit and crochet and even spin and weave, but they tend to do so as hobbies, often at considerable monetary expense and nearly always with a considerably greater investment of time than would have been required to purchase comparable goods at a store.

Sometimes, though, you cannot purchase what you need at a store. My husband can no longer find ready-made trousers to fit him. Faced with what we assumed would be the astronomical cost of tailor-made pants, I decided to haul out the sewing machine and give it a try. I had never constructed a fly before, but it turns out it's not too hard. Now every day, when my husband gets dressed in one or another of the pairs of trousers I have made—trousers that fit better than any he has had for years—he says to me, "I love these pants!"

At other times, handmade articles of clothing are simply different from the machine-made variety. I knitted a pair of socks recently, for the first time in a long time, and was reminded that hand-knitted socks are completely different from store-bought socks. Hand-knitted socks don't stretch. You just knit them the same size as your feet, and then you put your feet into them. Putting on a store-bought sock is like stuffing your foot into an elastic bandage; to put on a hand-knitted sock is to slip your foot into a garment crafted just for it.

More significantly, store-bought socks are just socks, whereas hand-knitted socks are an extension of the person who made them. There is something powerfully personal in making something for yourself, for a family member, for a friend, or for a stranger (like the infant layettes made by the women's guild at my church as gifts for poor mothers). When you knit a sock, you are not just knitting a sock; you are knitting yourself to the past and to the future and joining yourself to the person who will wear that sock.

There are, of course, other ways to join one life with another. Not everyone has to learn to knit or sew or spin. But there is something very real in the connections that are forged in handwork of various kinds, even when industrialization has changed the character of handwork from an art of necessity to an art of choice. People still live in their bodies, and there is still powerful significance to exercising one's body in knitting or sewing or weaving garments that will then clothe one's own body or the bodies of others.

Scripture employs metaphors of weaving and knitting to describe God's creation of our bodies. "Thou didst clothe me with skin and flesh," says Job, "and knit me together with bones and sinews" (10:11). "Thou didst form my inward parts, thou didst knit me together in my mother's womb," sings the psalmist (Psalm 139:13). The Israelite king Hezekiah, thinking himself on his deathbed, mourns, "Like a weaver I have rolled up my life; he cuts me off from the loom" (Isaiah 38:12).

In the New Testament, we see God's creation of the church described in similar terms. Christ is "the one Head, from whom the whole body, nourished and knit together through its joints and ligaments, grows with a growth that is from God" (Colossians 2:19). When the apostle Paul speaks of the church as "God's workmanship" (Ephesians 2:10), the image that arises before my eyes is that of God, seated at his loom, throwing the shuttle back and forth to the rhythmic clacking of the treadle as the pattern grows on the woven cloth.

Handwork is an art that binds people together across generations. Most people who learn to knit or sew are taught to do so by an older person, often a mother or another female relative. My mother taught me to use a sewing machine when I was seven, but somehow I had not learned to knit before I went to college. There, it seemed, everyone was knitting. I went home at Christmas and said, "Teach me to knit!" It turned out that my mother knitted in the German style, rather than the English style favored by most Americans. Now I, too, knit in that German style, as do the people whom I have since taught to knit.

The things we make can also form bridges between individuals and generations. Some of us have inherited beautiful textiles—a shawl, a sampler, a linen tablecloth or set of napkins. We would love to leave a similarly beautiful and personal legacy to our children and for this reason are drawn to handwork. As one woman who in recent years has taken up sewing says, "After all, what are you going to pass down to your daughter? A cell phone?"

But gifts of handwork need not be only for one's children. I have given two gifts that have been particularly meaningful to me (and, I hope, to their recipients): a sampler that I stitched as a wedding gift for a friend and a memorial sampler made for a different friend whose infant child had died. Each of these projects took quite some time to complete, and as I worked on them, a few minutes here and a few minutes there, I felt that my own joy in the one friend's circumstances and my sorrow in the other's were being sewn, stitch by stitch, into these samplers.

It is this capacity of handwork to make room for joy, room for grief, room for hope and waiting and process, that makes it so valuable a practice in a world that increasingly has no room for any of these things. Many of us have less and less experience with anything that unfolds over time; we expect everything to be instantaneous and are indignant when our e-mail takes more than two seconds to arrive in its recipients' in-boxes. But life is not instantaneous. It takes time, and handwork can be a way to weave temporality and process back into our lives. As one woman says, "Any knitter knows how it feels to pick up those needles at the beginning or at the end of the day and to create something while reflecting on our daily lives—stitch by stitch, thought by thought, moment by quiet moment."

Handwork can actually open up time, creating space for thoughts and words and relationships that might not otherwise find room to blossom. The wife of a pastor who served a rural parish relates how her husband liked to refinish furniture and would put an old chair in the trunk of the car when he made his pastoral calls. "He would sit outside near the barn where the farmer was working, or on a farm porch where the farmer's wife was knitting, quilting, or peeling apples, and talk to them while he sanded our chair." Instead of expecting his parishioners to stop working when he called, he joined them in work, their shared labors opening up a place for unhurried and unself-conscious pastoral conversation.

Whether we knit or sew, spin or weave, or refinish chairs, making things that people can use to clothe their bodies or furnish their homes can offer a welcome change from the recurring tasks of daily life. One woman says, "Whenever I begin to feel entangled and trapped in necessary tasks, I hear my grandmother's voice telling me that her mother used to admonish her: 'You have to make something, Sarah Elizabeth. You shouldn't spend all your time cooking and cleaning—those things are never done. You have to make something!'"

Cooking, cleaning, laundry—these things are necessary and important and perhaps more lasting, at least in their effects, than we tend to give them credit for. But it is important to make things too—things to wear and things to use, things to keep and things to give, things that can remind us of our own essential physicality and of our links to past and future generations.

5

Clothing a Household

———

O ne of my sisters-in-law tells a story about a time a few months after the birth of her first child. She was caring for the baby at home, and one day her husband came home from work and asked her what she had done that day. "I folded laundry," she said. It was at that instant she realized, she said, that as long as she stayed home, she was wasting her life, and she didn't want to do so for a second longer than she had to.

Not everyone is equally content to be home with small children, of course. But it is interesting that my sister-in-law's moment of insight ("I can't stand being home") came not as she thought about caring for the baby but as she thought about doing the laundry. Gather up the clothes from all over the house. Look at the stains; wonder if they can be gotten out. Wonder if it matters. Sort, wash, dry, fold. And then report at the end of the afternoon that this is how you spent your day.

Does it have to be this way? Is laundry so different from other kinds of work that it cannot be seen and experienced as worthwhile rather than worthless? Christian reflection on work emphasizes the value of work that serves the bodily necessities of those around us, the ways in which work can bring people together as they learn from and care for one another, and the pleasure in a job done well as people imitate God's own persistence in perfecting his creation. Can the work involved in clothing a household be a part of this?

For some people, sometimes it is. A recent article in my college alumnae magazine featured the responses of graduates to the question "What special talent or ability do you possess?" Amid responses detailing accomplishments ranging from motorcycle racing to tall-ship rigging, two in particular caught my eye. "Laundry is what I do better than anyone else," volunteered one woman. "I tell people I meet that I'm in 'textile management.'" Another described her ability to fold a king-size fitted sheet into a tidy square package. "I've often joked about putting it on my résumé."

To judge from the humorous and self-deprecating tones in which these two women speak of their laundry-related expertise, they are well aware that skills like these do not generally garner the kind of public admiration accorded to things like motorcycle racing or ship rigging. And yet even in their brief remarks there are hints of why these women find these everyday skills meaningful enough to call attention to them.

Both women talk about laundry in relational and intergenerational terms. The woman who folds sheets says she learned to do so from her mother (who, she reports, ironed the sheets before she folded them). The self-described textile manager credits her expertise to her three small children, who supply her with lots of material (so to speak) to work on. For both women, in other words, caring for clothing and household linens is a task that connects them with other people, both in their current relationships and as inheritors and practitioners of a traditional art.

The remarks of both women also suggest that these skills are ones that they have worked deliberately to develop and in which they take genuine satisfaction. The expert folder talks about how she started with twin-size sheets and worked up to king-size, "the ultimate folding challenge." The mother of three notes that while other people may accomplish great things in public life, "my kids' closets are the neatest on the planet, and their clothing has no spots!" Again, there is humor here, but there is something else too: the genuine pleasure that comes from doing something well.

In all of this there are echoes of the familiar themes of Christian theologies of work. Work connects people with their physical environments and with the other members of the communities of which they are a part, and gives them an opportunity to imitate and join with God in the various dimensions of God's own work. Clothing a household is like other kinds of work in all these respects. Most individual householders no longer make most articles of clothing, but the assembly of a wardrobe stocked with clothing or a linen closet stocked with sheets is still akin to the work of creation. Laundry is a work of providential care; mending is restorative or healing; ironing is an act of perfecting.

Even so seemingly nontranscendent an act as putting clothing away can be a gesture of memory or of hope. We put laundry away in drawers and closets in the expectation that another day or season will come when we will need these things again. We pack away baby clothes in boxes in the hope that another child or grandchild will be added to the family or that an opportunity will come to pass things along to others who will use them. We save articles of clothing that belonged to a loved one who has died, remembering the body that used to be clothed in these things and hoping for the day when our bodies and theirs will finally be truly, gloriously clothed.

Alongside all of this, of course, lies the reality of clothing as a simple necessity and the act of clothing others as a work of mercy. People have bodies, and our bodies need clothes. Our households thus need routines and practices that provide for these needs and for the needs of the house itself—sheets for the beds, towels for the bathrooms, a cloth for the dining table—routines rooted in the recognition that as we do such work, we are engaged in the essentials of life in the body and life in community.

CLOTHING

Clothing a household used to begin with a needle and thread. Well-to-do families employed a seamstress who came in regularly or occasionally to make new clothes for the family. Poorer women did their own sewing or served as seamstresses for others. Bedding and other household linens were hand-made, too—narrow widths of fabric were seamed together to make sheets, small pieces of cloth were pieced together and then quilted into bed coverings, fine and coarse fabrics were woven for formal and for daily use as table coverings and napkins.

The making of clothing and of household linens was time-consuming, which meant that the resulting items—clothes, sheets, tablecloths—were valuable possessions, scarce in all but the wealthiest households, and treated as a resource to be carefully conserved and passed down from one member of a family to another and from one generation to another. Even textiles so worn as to be unusable as clothing or bedding served a purpose, as testified by the rag rugs that adorned and insulated the floors of many a home.

Nowadays, most of us clothe our households not by making clothes but by purchasing them. This does not necessarily make the job easier. In households where money is scarce, it can be a real scramble, come winter, to see that every member of the household has a warm coat and boots. In households where money is plentiful, at least in relative terms, the challenges are often related more to managing abundance and choice. We may have more clothes than we know what to do with, as our bulging closets testify, and yet we may be tempted to come home with still more.

Where does this temptation come from? Why do people shop for clothes when they are pressed to find room for the clothes they already have? Shopping for clothing, as for other things, has in many instances come to resemble a kind of dazzling buffet party in which you wander through beautifully designed and brightly lit halls, feasting your eyes on the displays, fingering things, musing about what you might wear them with, and then, inevitably, purchasing things—because the only way to feel that you belong at this party is to keep on buying.

As Christians, we need an invitation to a different party. Perhaps we need an invitation to a different kind of event altogether. Not to a party at which the only requirement is that we come dressed in all our finery and prepared to acquire more of it, but to a pilgrimage. A pilgrimage is not an event; it is a journey. Clothes appropriate to a journey are not primarily for decoration or display. They are for comfort, for protection, for equipping. If you embark on a journey in clothing that is inappropriate or if you lug along things you don't need, it will be hard either to get to where you are going or to flourish along the way.

How much clothing does one really need for the pilgrimage that is the Christian life? Probably less than many of

us have. A closet organizer I know relates a story about helping a couple move into a new house with a walk-in closet.
The wife had twenty-two pairs of pajamas; the husband's suits
and shirts required nearly 20 feet of hanging space. Perhaps
not many people have acquired quite as many clothes as this,
but how many of us really need or wear all that we do have?

Joan Chittister, in a book of reflections on the Rule of
Saint Benedict, speaks of an annual discipline practiced in
years past by herself and her fellow Benedictine nuns. Every
Lenten season they would do an inventory of their goods and
clothing. "We wrote down 'five coifs, three scapulars, three
habits, seven books, one book bag' to determine where we
were slipping over into accumulation. It was a chastening
exercise."

Many of us might be chastened too if we were to pull
out of closets and drawers all of our clothes or all of the
clothes belonging to the members of our households and
made an inventory of them. But such an exercise could be a
step toward making clothing ourselves and our households
a more manageable and focused enterprise. It could be that
we have more things than we need and can conveniently take
care of and find room for.

What clothes we and our household members truly
need will depend on the shape of our particular pilgrimages.
Children need clothes for school and for play. Adults may
need formal or dressy clothes for work or for professional
activities. But as Chittister points out, "Weekly shopping
sprees and closets full of slightly worn silks are hardly necessary. A basic wardrobe and a few nice party things are surely
enough in a world where the poor have nothing and the rich
don't even remember what they do own."

The motif of pilgrimage can also be useful when we
think about how we acquire clothes for ourselves or the

members of our households. When people are on pilgrimage, they do not always have access to the ideal retail outlet at which to purchase ideal articles of clothing. Nor do they always have access to unlimited financial resources (or the illusion of such resources). When you are on pilgrimage, you tend to have to make do with what you have, and to help make that possible, you share what you have with your fellow pilgrims, and they with you.

I have an acquaintance, a retired woman who loves to travel, who once planned her trip of a lifetime, a cruise to Antarctica. She shopped and packed very carefully for this trip, in anticipation of all of the extreme weather she expected to encounter there. Then, somewhere between the hotel and the ship, her suitcase went missing. She was ready to go home right then. You can't go to Antarctica without clothes!

But her traveling companions rallied round her. Someone took her to the only store in the tiny town from which their ship was departing, and she bought some underthings. Someone else lent her some boots, someone else a coat, someone else a sweater and a pair of heavy pants. When the ship left port, she was on it. She spent that entire cruise wearing borrowed clothing, and to hear her tell the story, she felt richer for the experience, not poorer.

Most of us will never take a cruise to Antarctica. But I wonder how different this woman's experience was from those of us who find ourselves, one way or another, in the midst of communities of sharing. When my son was an infant, I was surprised to discover an underground economy of baby clothes in which neither I nor anyone I knew ever bought anything. We just gave things to one another, used them for as long as we needed them, and then passed them along to someone else.

It is more difficult to do this as children get older and wear their clothes longer and harder. And it is harder still with adults' clothing, given the disparities of size and style. Still, places like charity shops and thrift stores provide a way to share clothing, if not with people we know, then with people we don't. When we inventory our closets we may discover clothes that, to paraphrase the Catholic social activist Dorothy Day, should be not in our closets but on someone else's back. A trip to the local secondhand clothing store may be in order as we pass these clothes on to people who need them.

Alternatively, we may find that there are things we or our fellow household members do not have and truly need. Perhaps our children are growing out of their clothes. Perhaps our own wardrobes require some updating or expanding. Buying clothing that is used rather than new can be a way to excuse ourselves from the glitzy party that so much of contemporary shopping has become while affirming our membership in the broader human community, in which if we share with one another, we can all be decently clad.

LAUNDRY

In the days before running water, clothes washing was an enormously labor-intensive chore, one that involved the transfer of hundreds of pounds of water from pump to bucket to washtub and of equally heavy loads of dripping-wet laundry from washtub to rinse water to laundry basket to clothesline. The days-of-the-week housework rhymes that many of us learned when we were children may have varied in the jobs they assigned toward the end of the week, but they all began the same way: "Wash on Monday." Washing was so backbreaking a job that the housewife and her helpers needed their Sabbath rest before beginning the laundry.

In these days of automatic washing machines, the challenges of laundry have shifted: gaining access to a machine (your own or someone else's), making the time actually to do the laundry (since even an "automatic" machine does not in fact run itself), and imposing enough structure on the task so that it does not completely take over your life. Most of us are glad to have the flexibility that comes with not having to devote one entire day per week to laundry, but finding oneself doing the wash at all hours of the day and night is not necessarily an improvement.

Of course there can be real convenience in being able to put a load of laundry in sometime in the evening, stay up just late enough to transfer it to the dryer, and wake up in the morning to clean, dry clothes. Laundromats stay open late in the evening or even around the clock to offer similar convenience to people who do not have their own washer-dryers. And yet the ability to do the laundry at odd hours can fuel an inclination to regard laundry as a negligible task, one to be fit into odd moments here and there, as distinct from the truly important work that we give our daylight hours to.

It can be a short step from fitting the laundry in here and there to not fitting it in, resenting the fact that the dirty clothes are piling up, and finding oneself (and the other members of one's household) without anything to wear. Laundry may no longer be as physically demanding a task as it was in past ages, but it is still time-consuming and needs to be deliberately woven into the structures of our days and weeks. Establishing a regular pattern for the wash can help us experience this work not as "time-consuming" so much as "clean clothes–producing" and thus as a task whose rewards are proportionate to the effort we put into it.

When I was a child, I was taught to sort the laundry— darks in one pile, whites in another, bright colors in yet another. Whites were to be washed in hot water, darks in cold, colors in warm. This way, I was advised, fabrics would not shrink and colors would not bleed or fade. None of these reasons really survives as a reason to sort the laundry. Modern fabrics, dyes, and detergents conspire together to make pretty much everything pretty much indestructible. You do still get less light lint on dark things if you sort, so that is one practical reason to continue to do so.

But more than that, sorting provides an anticipation of order in doing the laundry. If you just pull off the top of the pile and throw it in the machine, the process is endless. But if you gather every piece of dirty laundry from all over the house, put it in one big pile on the floor, and then sort it into however many load-size piles, by color (lights, darks, brights) or by item (jeans and pants in one load, shirts and socks in another, towels in another) you begin to bring order, even before the laundry is done. It is both relaxing and energizing to have such order not just at the end of the job but in the midst of it. And it is much more pleasant to fold laundry that has been sorted before being washed—it is so much less miscellaneous than unsorted laundry.

Of course there are times when you are not doing so much wash that you can have lots of meticulously sorted loads. There are bound to be days when there are a few dark things and a few light things that you have to have clean for tomorrow, and there is no time to do two loads, and it would waste water and electricity to do so few clothes in two loads anyway, so you throw them in together and hope for the best.

There is a time for not caring or for realizing that this doesn't really matter right now. But the time for not caring is when there is less laundry, not more. The bigger the job, the more it needs internal structure to be manageable and pleasant.

As in so many things nowadays, there is a siren song sung by technology when it comes to laundry. Washing machines are sold not simply as tools to get the job done but as consumer goods in their own right. I once read a newspaper article headlined "Laundry Lust" that detailed the desire for high-end laundry machines, complete with photographs of fancy laundry rooms owned by wealthy people who actually send their laundry out. But even for people who expect to use their washing machines, it is no longer assumed that it is enough that the machine should simply wash the clothes. On the contrary, say the advertising copywriters for one luxury brand of washing machine: "Your clothes deserve expert care and high-performance cleaning."

The fact is, if your washing machine works at all, it probably works well enough to get your laundry passably clean. And on the lower end of the income spectrum, having a washing machine that works is challenge enough. When I was a graduate student, I lived in an apartment complex that had a communal laundry room that was shared by all the buildings in the complex. The fact that hundreds of people were using these twenty or so washing machines probably accounted for a large part of the reason that most of them were usually broken. One day the scene in the laundry room was so demoralizing, with practically every machine either flooded or smoking, that I walked out and never went back.

At that point in my life, I couldn't face another laundromat, even a (possibly better-run) commercial one. But I had friends who owned their own washing machine, which they kept in a basement with an exterior entrance that they did not lock. For the next several years, I drove across town with my laundry and washed it in my friends' machine. My friends also had an automatic clothes dryer, but I did not want to spend entire afternoons sitting in their basement waiting for several loads of laundry to dry. So I would drive back home with the wet wash and hang it on the line behind my apartment (the clothesline being the only part of the communal laundry facility that actually worked).

In ways I hardly noticed at the time, those laundry arrangements wove community and relationality into my household life. I was newly widowed and deep in the sorrow and isolation of grief. It didn't seem, many mornings, as if there was much to get up for. But if, when I opened my eyes, I saw the sun, my first thought was, "Laundry!" I would drive to my friends' house and do the wash in their basement, grateful for their hospitality even if they happened not to be home. And then I would take the laundry back with me and pin it out, beginning, in that small way, to connect again with the world beyond my household and its particularities and losses.

Hanging out the laundry may be impracticable for many people. You may live in the city with nowhere to put a clothesline. You may live in one of the increasing number of suburban developments that ban clotheslines (itself a very interesting attempt at suppressing the reality of housework and detaching people from their natural environments). You may live in a climate in which good line-drying days are rare. Or you may simply work full time at a job that precludes the kind of flexibility necessary to respond to beautiful weather by doing laundry.

But if you work flexible hours or are at home and if you have a place to put a clothesline, why not hang the laundry out? So much of modern life is disconnected from the world beyond our doors. People go to work or to school whether it rains or shines; they exercise indoors on stationary bicycles rather than riding outdoors on real bicycles. Hanging out the wash can be one small way to begin living in response to and in cooperation with the natural world, receiving both rain and sun as gifts from the God who made both us and our world.

MENDING AND IRONING

Mending and ironing are the backwaters of the laundry cycle. Put a shirt into the ironing basket, and it might not see the light of day for weeks. Put it in the mending basket, and you might as well have put it in the garbage. The garbage is where lots of clothes that need mending do in fact end up. One woman explains the process this way: "I never mend. When a button comes off something, I put the button in a safe place and lay the garment across the back of a chair, so I won't forget. When there are enough things piled on the chair to be inconvenient, I throw them away."

Our mothers and grandmothers, many of whom could darn a sock and turn a collar, would no doubt be horrified. But there are reasons for the decline of mending as a practical art, central among which is the fact that in modern industrialized societies, clothing is so abundant and so cheap. Why should anyone mend, when new (or secondhand) clothing is so inexpensive? I recently purchased a pair of iron-on patches with which to mend the knees of a pair of my son's blue jeans. I buy most of his clothes on clearance, and the patches cost about half of what I have sometimes spent on a brand-new pair of pants. And then it took a half an hour to mend the jeans. Was it really worth it?

The tension between mending and throwing things out can become something of a practical and ethical dilemma. Contributors to Internet discussion groups reveal both a settled conviction that mending is not something the writers are willing to do and a guilty sense that it would be a shame to throw out clothes that "only" need to be mended. "It seems like such a waste to make scraps out of them," sighs one writer, describing a pair of leggings with a hole in the knee. "No, I won't get around to patching it. I should, but I admit that I just don't have time to mend."

The solution, as suggested by another contributor to the discussion, is to give away the unmended clothes to a local service that collects such things. "Put the items in a sturdy garbage bag; label visibly, 'You Are Special.' These items go to help families who are desperate. You can send pants with a hole in the knee." The irony, of course, is all too obvious. What person is going to feel "special" upon being given clothes with holes in them? Slightly less naked, perhaps; special, no. And yet many of us can sympathize, at least, with the feeling that surely there must be someone out there who can use what we can no longer use, who will fix what we cannot or will not fix, who can take the dregs of our abundance and thus free us from the guilt that comes from seeing perhaps too clearly that we have more things than we can even comfortably dispose of.

Mending alone is not going to solve the problem of overconsumption, either in the culture at large or among Christians. Some kinds of mending are not even possible any more. Socks machine-made of modern fibers cannot be darned because the socks are stretchy and a darn would not be. When your children's socks get holes in them, there is no point in feeling guilty because your grandmother would have darned them but you never learned how. Even Grandmother couldn't have darned these socks. They are through being socks, although they might find a new purpose as rags.

There are kinds of mending, though, that are worth doing. When a button falls off, a seam rips, a thread snags, or a hem comes down, mending can be a way to affirm that just because something is broken does not mean it cannot be fixed. It isn't just our garments that we are tempted to throw out at the first indication of imperfection; it is many other things too, up to and including our relationships with other people. Perhaps if we are willing to take the time to mend our clothes, we will develop the discipline and patience we need to mend other things as well.

Mending can even be creative. I once took a pair of children's winter pajamas that had an enormous, unfixable hole in the knee, cut off the legs and sleeves, hemmed them all up, and turned them into summer pajamas. I was as proud of those pajamas as if I had made them myself. I hadn't just given an old garment a longer life. It seemed as if I had made a whole new garment. In a world in which the first step in almost any process is to go to the store, it can be a welcome relief to make something that starts only with what we already have on hand and turn it into something new.

Ironing is another traditional practice that in modern times has retreated to the edges of household work. We need look no further for evidence of this than to the emergence of the so-called sport of "extreme ironing," in which people iron while hang gliding or mountain climbing. No one makes an extreme sport out of something they think is actually necessary, like emptying the wastebaskets. And in fact it is perfectly possible nowadays to get by without ironing at all— lots of clothing is made of no-iron fabrics, there are commercial laundries that will wash and iron things that do need ironing, few of us do the kind of entertaining that requires ironed tablecloths or napkins, and nobody expects ironed sheets or pillowcases anymore.

So why can it seem, as a friend of mine once said, that "ironing really is a result of the Fall"? Perhaps it is because the less absolutely or universally necessary something becomes, the more of an imposition it seems on the occasions when it does appear to need to be done. If most clothing doesn't have to be ironed, why should this shirt require ironing? And why should it be the favorite shirt of its owner, so that the instant it is ironed, it gets worn, only to end up back in the dirty-clothes hamper and shortly thereafter in the ironing basket?

Although I fall as behind in it as anyone, I have actually always rather enjoyed ironing. The Canadian writer Molly Wolf talks about certain categories of household work as being conducive to "Martha-prayer," which she defines as "the contemplation possible when the hands are busy." For me, ironing is high on the list of such tasks. It requires attention but not thought and so leaves the heart free to meditate on whatever comes to mind, all while the hands go through the familiar steps involved in turning wrinkly things into smooth things.

And there is a kind of perfection that ironing serves. Linen tea towels dry the dishes just as well unironed as ironed, but they lie stacked on the shelf and hang over the oven door handle so much more nicely if they have been ironed. Permanent-press shirts may not really have to be ironed, but they look nicer if they are. All things being equal, I would rather take the time to iron the shirts, so I can put them away in a nice crisp row in the closet, rather than just hanging them up limply as they come out of the dryer or off the clothesline.

Of course, things are not always equal. I started out
ironing my first husband's shirts partly because I liked doing
it and partly because I assumed he would like it too. It turned
out that he had strong opinions about efficiency and thought
ironing permanent-press shirts was highly inefficient. He was
actually more pleased when I didn't iron his shirts than when
I did. When I married my second husband, I started out ironing his shirts too. He was delighted, as he really did prefer
ironed shirts and for various reasons couldn't iron them himself. But he is very tall and his shirts are very big, and the cuffs
would drag on the floor and get dirty while I was ironing unless the floor was very clean, which it never was because we
had two dogs and a baby. Finally I saw the light and began
sending his shirts out.

I still do get out the ironing board occasionally and
work my way through various wrinkly things. The other day
I washed and ironed some curtains and put them back up
again. They had been looking rather limp and dusty for some
time, and as I pressed them smooth and flat, I felt that
some small but real measure of beauty and order was in process of being restored to them and to the bedroom in which
they had hung. Now when I see those curtains hanging
crisply at the window, I think, "There's a job well done!"

PUTTING THINGS AWAY

Jesus speaks in one of his parables of a rich man whose land
produced so much grain that he had nowhere to put it. "He
thought to himself, 'What shall I do, for I have nowhere to
store my crops?'" So the man decided to pull down his barns
and build larger ones in which he could store all his grain and

his goods and so feel secure in the knowledge that he had enough to last him for many years. We know how the story ends: that night God said to the rich man, "'Fool! This night your soul is required of you; and the things you have prepared, whose will they be?'" So is the person, Jesus says, who lays up treasure for himself and is not rich toward God. Don't worry about what you will wear, for the body is more than clothing, and God will clothe you as he clothes the lilies of the field (Luke 12:13–28).

In a culture in which the closet has become, in the words of one commentator, "a paean to our possessions," these words of Jesus are surely enough to give one pause. American home architecture has entered the age of the closet. In the 1800s closets were taxed as rooms, inspiring householders to store their clothes in armoires or chests instead. By the early 1900s houses had closets, but they were modest affairs, like the bungalow closets novelist Ann Patchett remembers from her childhood: "a little slot in the wall meant to hold the four suits or five dresses one owned."

Now, in the early twenty-first century, multiple walk-in closets are featured in virtually all new homes. Entire industries exist to assist people in organizing their closets and in housing the overflow of their possessions that won't fit in the closets. We might need these things sometime, we think; we'll be glad someday that we kept them. And then we sigh as we look for a place to put the folded laundry, because all the drawers are already full to overflowing.

Perhaps one of the first things to consider, as we go to put things away, is how we might manage with the space we have. Patchett, who has long lived in houses with multiple large closets, asks, "I wonder if I could make it in a bungalow now. . . . I wonder if, instead of having a closet that was designed to fit my life, I could once again design my life to fit into the closet." Can we fit our lives, and our clothes, into the closets we have, rather than seeking somehow to expand the closet to accommodate our ever-expanding wardrobes?

I live in an old house with few and tiny closets. Part of the reason I find it hard to put things away is that there really isn't much place to put them. But part of the problem too is that much of the existing closet space is taken up with things I seldom wear, leaving the often worn items to swirl around on the surface with nowhere to settle down. Periodically I have to empty the closets of less used things to make that space available for the clothing that I and the members of my household actually wear.

And it is important to put things away. Putting away things that get daily or weekly use is a way to exercise a kind of providential foresight. We will, in fact, need these things. Every morning, people need something to put on. Having clothes ready to wear in the drawer or in the closet is part of creating an expectation that in this home we care for one another. Our needs are not a perpetual emergency but are anticipated and provided for ahead of time as a matter of course.

Sometimes clothes need to be put away for longer periods of time. Seasons change, and clothing with them. When winter gives way to spring or summer to fall, it is time to get out boxes, to unpack things set aside half a year ago and to pack away things that will not be worn until the seasons turn again. The changing of the seasons can provide a natural opportunity to go through our own or others' clothing and decide what should be saved to wear again next year and what should be given away as no longer suitable or necessary.

Children get bigger, and their clothes have to be put away for the next child in line. When there are no younger children in the household, the question becomes "Might there be?" Do we save these things, hoping there will be another child? Or do we give them away, recognizing that there likely will not be? Perhaps we are content for this child to be the last; perhaps we wish there could be more. In either case, we are reminded of the fact that we do not make the future but receive it as a gift. We have our expectations and our plans, but it is God who holds us in the palm of his hand.

Some things we may save more with an eye to the past than to the future. A few months after my first husband died, I gave away most of his clothes. After all, what would I have done with them? Better that someone else should have the use of them. But I kept his formal clothes: his tuxedo, his tailcoat, his pleated shirts and vests and cummerbunds and ties. He was a musician, and those clothes were so tied up with who he was and who he had been to me that I could not bear to let them go.

I still have them. Unlike the books and other possessions that I kept, all of which have now been mine for so long that I have more or less forgotten that they were first his, those clothes will never be mine. Perhaps one day they will fit one of his nephews, and then I will hand them down, as I did his other clothes so many years ago. Or perhaps they will just continue to hang in the back of the closet, a small, tactile reminder of a past life, a great sorrow, a hope for the day when God will clothe us all anew.

Of course, most of us are not thinking in such cosmic and eschatological terms as we go about the task of clothing our households. We are trying to get our children or spouses to put their dirty clothes in the hamper rather than on the floor, trying to get a load of wash in before we start dinner, trying to find that lost sock or that missing button. And yet clothing is so basic a reality that simply making sure everyone has something to wear can be a powerful way of making a home a nurturing and hospitable place, a place that helps us remember that we are all on pilgrimage together.

6

Food to Eat

Evelyn Birkby was an Iowa farm wife who in the 1940s and 1950s wrote a weekly newspaper column about farm life. The editor who hired her advised her to include a recipe in every column, and so she did. Recalling this fifty years later, Mrs. Birkby said, "It was good advice. Food is so daily." Food is indeed daily. Jesus himself, as he taught his disciples to pray for daily bread, acknowledged as much. One of the fundamental characteristics of humans' embodied nature is that people need to eat, and they need to eat every day.

Christian scripture embraces this necessity, portraying food and eating as central to God's plan for his creation from beginning to end. God planted the Garden of Eden with "every tree that is pleasant to the sight and good for food" (Genesis 2:9). When God rescues his people from captivity in Egypt, he leads them into "a land flowing with milk and honey" (Exodus 3:8). In the New Testament, the experience of redemption itself is described as a meal: "Blessed are those who are invited to the marriage supper of the Lamb," writes the author of the book of Revelation (19:9).

Things that are central to God's original purposes in creation and to God's ultimate purposes in redemption usually

turn out to be among the things that are most seriously affected by humans' sin and its tragic consequences in the world
around them. Food is no exception. The author of the book of
Genesis tells us that it was through eating a food that God had
forbidden to them that Adam and Eve brought sin into the
world. Our first parents could have honored God by heeding
this, the sole prohibition in the midst of the abundance God
laid before them. Instead, they ate what was not theirs to eat
and set in motion a whole range of tragic consequences.

Chief among those consequences was a change in humans' relationship to food itself. "Cursed is the ground because of you," God said to Adam. "In toil you shall eat of it
all the days of your life; thorns and thistles it shall bring forth
to you. . . . In the sweat of your face you shall eat bread. . ."
(Genesis 3:17–19). Famine became a dreaded reality. It was
because of a famine in the land of Canaan that Jacob's sons
took up residence in Egypt, where their descendants became
slaves of the Egyptians. When the prophets took Israel to task
for its unfaithfulness, famine was among the punishments from
God that they predicted would befall it.

The prophets hoped for a day when famine would be
reversed and plenty would be restored. In the ministry of
Jesus, this day begins to arrive. Jesus' first miracle, at the wedding at Cana, involves the transformation of water into wine—
a remedy of an awkward social situation, yes, but more than
that an outpouring of abundance in the face of want. Later
in his ministry Jesus is teaching thousands of people and they
all get hungry. There appears at first not to be enough food.
But then Jesus takes a child's gift of five barley loaves and
two fishes and distributes them, and when everyone has
eaten his fill, the disciples gather up twelve baskets of leftovers. Jesus, evidently, is a host at whose table there is always
enough and more.

Food is not just abundant in the ministry of Jesus; it is community-building and revelatory. Jesus does not only feed people. He sits down and eats with them, and every time he does, we learn something about who Jesus is or who his companions are (or both). Jesus eats with tax collectors and sinners, and when his motives for doing so are questioned, he replies, "I came to call not the righteous, but sinners" (Luke 5:32). Jesus gives his ministry and his presence to those who need him, and the sinners with whom he eats are destined to be recipients of his healing grace.

The Passover meal that Jesus shares with his disciples is likewise revelatory, but sadly so. "He who has dipped his hand in the dish with me, will betray me," Jesus tells his friends sorrowfully (Matthew 26:23). Blessing comes through this meal too, though, as Jesus establishes the common meal that has come to mark the communal life of his followers ever since. "As they were eating, Jesus took bread, and blessed, and broke it, and gave it to the disciples and said, 'Take, eat; this is my body'" (Matthew 26:26). For two millennia now, Christians have been breaking bread and blessing it and expecting as they do so to encounter Jesus and feed upon him.

Throughout his teaching, Jesus uses food and feeding others as images of what it means to follow Jesus and to serve him well. "Who then is the faithful and wise servant, whom his master has set over his household, to give them their food at the proper time?" Jesus asks his disciples. "Blessed is that servant whom his master when he comes will find so doing" (Matthew 24:45). Serving God faithfully, these words suggest, is like feeding a household; it is a daily responsibility that requires attention and diligence and that brings blessing on the one who does it faithfully.

Jesus goes so far as to suggest that there is something redemptive about the very act of feeding the hungry. When the

Son of Man comes in his glory, he says, he will separate the people one from another as a shepherd separates sheep and goats, and the sheep he will invite into the kingdom, saying to them, "I was hungry and you gave me food, I was thirsty and you gave me drink." "But when did we do this?" they will ask. "And the King will answer them, 'Truly, I say to you, as you did it to one of the least of these my brethren, you did it to me'" (Matthew 25:40).

Words like these suggest that food and eating, feeding others and eating with them, are central to the kingdom of God itself. They show us who Jesus is, who our neighbor is, and who we are in relation to them. If this is so, surely these things should also be central to the lives of Christian individuals and Christian households as we all seek together to live in ways that are appropriate for members of the household of God.

GOOD EATING

A great deal of contemporary cultural concern about food focuses on what we eat. How we eat, though, is at least as significant a subject. By this I do not mean whether we use forks or chopsticks or whether we follow the advice supposedly offered by a nineteenth-century dietary reformer that we chew each bite of food one hundred times. Rather, I mean to focus attention on a few of the most basic structures and attitudes that underlie the practices of eating and feeding one another, particularly as these are illuminated by Christian scripture and tradition.

In the first place, good eating is characterized by routine and predictability. People get hungry every day, and they need to be fed every day. Meals may follow the familiar pattern of breakfast, lunch, and dinner. At some times and places other patterns have prevailed. Saint Benedict, who in the sixth century founded a monastery and wrote a rule to order its common life, directed that the monks should have two meals a day in summer (when days were long and filled with labor in the fields) and one meal a day in winter (when days were shorter and spent mostly indoors).

Benedict founded his monastery at a time of considerable political and social instability in Italy. The order grew rapidly, and it has been suggested that in addition to the spiritual vocation undoubtedly sensed by most members, a further motivation for joining the order may have been the monastery's reliable provision of the basic necessities of life, including regular meals. Few crises compare with being hungry and having nothing to eat, and few acts of care compare with being fed when one is hungry.

In the modern American culture, in which "busyness" can seem simultaneously like the badge of a good life and like a curse that is impossible to escape, finding time to eat or to feed others can become a challenge. People eat on the run; they feed their children in the car; they skip breakfast, eat lunch at their desks, and panic when it is dinnertime. Magazine headlines in the grocery store checkout aisle ("From Desperation to Dinner in 15 Minutes!") suggest that in too many households, the need of people for an evening meal has become a perpetual emergency.

In contrast to this stand biblical stories like that of the manna in the wilderness. Manna was not, perhaps, the most exciting thing the people of Israel had ever eaten (indeed, there came a point at which they complained bitterly about it), but it was palatable and it was predictable. It was there every day, in a quantity sufficient for the day (and on the eve of the Sabbath, enough for two days), and through that reliable daily provision

God's people were sustained. We too need to meet the predictable hunger of our households with a predictable provision
of food. The food doesn't have to be fancy, necessarily, or even
particularly varied. But it needs to be there, in the cupboard or
the refrigerator, so that when mealtime rolls around, what en-
sues is not panic but dinner.

Good eating is also rhythmic or structured. It is not all
food, all the time, but rather particular foods at particular
times. Scripture portrays this as having been God's intention
even in Eden, where our first parents were told they could eat
of the fruit of all the trees in the garden but one. As the law
developed among the people of Israel, a great many laws had
to do with practices restricting and thus structuring food and
eating—when people were to eat, when they were to fast,
when they were to abstain from particular foods, what foods
they were not to eat at all.

In the life of the early church, a significant subject of
conversation concerned whether and to what degree the
dietary restrictions of the Old Covenant bound Christian believers under the New Covenant. The apostle Peter, who had
hesitated to eat foods that Jewish law defined as "unclean,"
was persuaded by a dream (Acts 10:9–16) that all foods were
now clean. The author of the gospel of Mark traces this development to the teaching of Jesus himself, and Jesus' decla-
ration that it is what comes out of a person that can defile
him, not anything that goes into a person (Mark 7:18–19).

And yet early Christians did not take this new dietary
freedom as license to eat anything, anytime. The apostles and
other elders assembled at the Council of Jerusalem ruled that
Christians should abstain "from what is strangled and from
blood" (Acts 15:20). The apostle Paul distinguished between
what was lawful and what was helpful in discussing whether
Christians could eat meat that might have been slaughtered in

conjunction with pagan sacrifice (1 Corinthians 10:23–33). In the era immediately following that of the New Testament, the early Christian manual of discipline called the Didache called on Christians to distinguish themselves from the Jews not by rejecting the Jewish practice of fasting but by fasting on Wednesdays and Fridays rather than the Mondays and Thursdays preferred by other groups.

In other words, Christians' attitudes toward eating have from the beginning been marked by the conviction that good eating is a structured and disciplined practice, in which not eating some things at some times is just as significant as what one does eat. Eating and not eating are related, just as sound and silence are related in the making of music. If you have only sound, then what you have is not music but cacophony. You need silence too, at least in some of the voices some of the time, if you are to have music. Good eating likewise requires that at least some of the time we not eat, and that we make a habit of eating moderately rather than to excess.

This is not, perhaps, as simple as it might sound. In our culture, many people feel they do not have time to stop and eat, so instead they eat and drink continuously, grazing on one or another of the increasing number of foods that come packaged in squeezable tubes or in containers designed to fit in the cupholders of their cars or strollers. And while many people voice a concern about the potential consequences of overeating, restaurants and food companies appear to be extremely successful in attracting customers with the offer of enormous servings of food and drink.

The ancient Christian practice of structuring eating according to weekly and yearly patterns of feast days, fast days, and ordinary days can be helpful as we think about how to structure our own patterns of eating and of feeding our households. There are weekly feast days—namely, Sundays—and yearly days and seasons of feasting, like Christmas and Easter. There are weekly fast days—Friday is the most broadly observed such day—and yearly periods of fasting, most notably Lent. And then there are all the other days, the weekdays that are neither feast days nor fast days.

We may observe or adapt these practices in a variety of ways. Perhaps Sunday will be a day when someone who likes to cook devotes extra time to preparing a special meal to be shared by household members and perhaps by guests as well. Alternatively, Sunday may be a day when the household eats particularly simple food so as to give the cook a day of rest.

I have acquaintances who chose to make Sunday a day both of simple food and of hospitality. Every week they would invite a number of young people from church to share their Sunday lunch, and every week they would serve grilled cheese sandwiches. No one ever complained about the food; on the contrary, the friends gathered round their table basked in the warmth of their hospitality and counted the days until they could come again.

Fast days, in their turn, can be an opportunity to back away, if only in a small way, from the seemingly unlimited abundance of modern American culture and the modern American supermarket. Perhaps this will mean abstention from particular foods, like meat or sweets; perhaps it will mean the eating of smaller or fewer meals. In the Christian tradition, not only Lent but Advent as well is understood as a season of penitence and fasting. In the midst of the frantic busyness of the commercial holiday season, the deliberate preparation and sharing of small and simple meals can help make a place for the watchful waiting that is Advent and to open the way to a truly joyful celebration of the Christmas feast.

And then there are the ordinary days, the ferial days as they are sometimes called—weekdays that are neither feasts nor fasts. These days are the norm from which feast days and fast days deviate, days on which we eat ordinary foods in ordinary amounts at ordinary times. These are the days that can too easily be squeezed out of existence by the pressures of everyday life as we lurch from overindulging to not having time to eat. But it is worth making the effort to structure our household routines so that they include regular meals at regular times, precisely so that our practices of eating and of feeding one another have a center of gravity that can help anchor our common lives.

And finally, good eating is characterized by gratitude. It is eucharistic, in the broadest sense of the term. Jesus is recorded in scripture as giving thanks before meals (John 6:11), as is the apostle Paul (Acts 27:35), and Christians in all walks of life have long been in the habit of "saying grace" as one means of expressing thanks to God as he sustains our lives through gifts of food.

Many Christians today continue the practice of saying grace, and many more would readily agree that thankfulness is a proper attitude with which to receive one's daily bread. But the prevalence of ads for food and food supplements or substitutes that emphasize speed and convenience above all else suggest that for many modern people, impatience may be more fundamental. It can be easy to find ourselves resenting the time that it takes to shop for food, to cook, to eat, to clean up. But it can be precisely as we resist our culture's encouragement to rush through preparing and eating food and instead take the time to cook and to eat that we show our thankfulness for daily bread, even as we may also say our thanks before we partake.

GOOD FOOD

There is another dimension to the eucharistic reception of food. If we are truly to be thankful for the food we eat, we have to believe that the food itself is good. But the goodness of food, and in particular the question of whether any particular food may be "good for you," is hardly assumed in much of modern American culture. On the contrary: it seems that food is often viewed not as a friend but as an enemy, something against whose potential ill effects one must be on guard at all times.

A generation ago, Robert Farrar Capon wrote a simultaneously funny and pointed commentary about people who viewed all food as agglomerations of calories and would eat or refuse food based not on whether the food was well prepared and delicious but on whether or not they had met their calorie quota for the day. The result was that they would eat packaged doughnuts for breakfast but would refuse homemade noodles at dinner.

In our day, the calorie has been joined by a host of other gremlins—fat grams, trans fats, carbs, free radicals—but the result is the same. I once took a loaf of homemade Swedish coffee bread to a meeting. After the meeting I offered a leftover piece to a wafer-thin colleague whom I encountered in the hallway. She turned pale, said, "Think of the fat and the sugar!" and fled. I am sure she would have said the same thing had I offered her a Twinkie—failing, in other words, to recognize the complete and decisive difference between Twinkies and homemade Swedish coffee bread.

How are we to tell the difference between good food and bad food? If a starving person were offered a Twinkie, he or she would do well to eat it, as something is undoubtedly better than nothing. But most of us have choices about what we eat, and the challenge is in deciding what to choose. Contemporary fears about carbs and trans fats have this to be said for them: they offer a way to winnow the choices available to one. But are there more discernibly Christian criteria for determining what counts as good food and thus narrowing the field from which we make our food choices?

One such criterion ought surely to have to do with the ways in which food is produced. No gift can be received with thankfulness if the giver is being treated disrespectfully or abusively. This is as true of food as it is of any other gift. But a great deal of food production in the developed world is anything but respectful of the people or animals or even the land that provides that food.

Perhaps the most striking instance of such disrespect is the treatment of animals in factory farms. It used to be that yields of meat and milk and eggs were highest when animals were treated well—when, for example, they were kept healthy by being kept clean and were allowed to engage in natural behaviors like grazing and sleeping. What was good for the animal, in other words, was good for the farmer and for those who purchased the farmer's produce.

Sadly, this is so no longer. Meat and milk and eggs can be produced in greater quantity at lower cost if the animals involved are crowded into pens too small for them to move around in, fed food laced with animal by-products and antibiotics, kept awake with continuous bright lights so they will eat more and thus grow faster, and prevented from destroying one another in these unbearable conditions by the amputation of beaks and tails. As horrific as all this sounds (and is), it is tolerated and even encouraged by the culture at large because it results in cheap, abundant food.

There are numbers of people, both Christian and non-Christian, who have suggested that the most moral response to the problem of agricultural animal abuse is a vegetarian diet. Among Christians, this argument is often bolstered by contentions that the original human diet was vegetarian, the Eucharist is vegetarian, and the heavenly banquet will be vegetarian. As one advocate of such a position puts it, "Every meal should anticipate the heavenly banquet of the peaceable kingdom, where everyone will have enough to eat and no blood is shed."

I don't find this a persuasive argument, at least in principle. Perhaps the supper of the Lamb is a vegetarian feast, but that cannot ipso facto imply that all Christians are to be vegetarians in their earthly lives. There is no marriage or giving in marriage in heaven, but that does not mean that Christians are not to marry in this life or that marriage is somehow second-best. Some are called to matrimony and some to celibacy, and both are equally valid and valuable ways to serve and follow God. So also with matters related to diet. Some may choose to be vegetarians. Others may choose to eat meat. Both are choices with moral resonance, and either can be a good choice.

But whatever we eat, we need to consider where it comes from, and how the animals—and humans—involved in its production were treated. Could we look them in the eye and say thank-you without being ashamed? The eighteenth-century Quaker John Woolman found that he could not do this where slaves were concerned. He began paying others' slaves for any personal services they might perform for him and eventually refused to eat food grown by slaves or wear clothes made from cloth dyed by slaves. Woolman became one of the most influential abolitionists of his day, arguing that the slave system as a whole was an affront to the humanity of slaves and to the light of Christ that God had placed in them.

Questions of food production carry similar moral weight in the modern period. Slavery was held dear by its practitioners in part because it was seen as a source of cheap abundance. Both labor and commodities were cheaper with an enslaved workforce. In our day, the cheapest meat comes from factory farms and the cheapest produce is harvested by desperately poor migrants on enormous monoculture farms. Are we willing to spend more, or eat less, at least of certain things at certain times in order to lessen the degree of our collusion with such a system and perhaps contribute to its eventual demise?

Another way to think about the difference between good food and bad is to consider whether and in what ways food connects us with the times and places in which we live. The fallen condition of humans is sometimes described as one of alienation. Human beings, who were created to live in harmony with each other, the earth, and God, now find themselves distanced from or at odds with their fellow humans, their physical surroundings, and their Lord. Redemption, then, consists in healing these breaches and restoring right relationships among all of these parties.

The things we eat play a part in this. The contemporary American diet is too often a case study in alienation, consisting as it does of foods that come from all over the world and are available all of the time. This may seem counterintuitive—shouldn't such a diet make people more connected to more of their surroundings? But just as global communication technologies erode the time people spend talking in person to people they actually know, so the constant availability of foods from all over the world erodes the connection people have to their own local environment and the foods associated with it.

Gary Paul Nabham, in his book *Coming Home to Eat,* talks about the significance of what he calls "unplugging the global vending machine." Going to the supermarket is too often akin to using a vending machine: you put in a quarter, and out tumbles, say, asparagus from Chile. But when April rolls around, is there local asparagus in the market? Probably not—because it is easier and cheaper for the market to buy its asparagus from Chile year round, regardless of what is in season locally. And in the meantime, people forget the flavor of truly fresh asparagus and forgo the pleasure and connection of eating what is in season precisely because it is in season.

Contemporary technologies of food storage and transportation are things we can all be thankful for; they allow a far more varied and in many cases more nutritious diet than was enjoyed by many of our forebears. But we can be even more thankful for fresh local foods in season. Asparagus, strawberries, and peas in spring; beans, tomatoes, and corn in summer; apples, pumpkins, and broccoli in fall; cabbage, beets, and potatoes in winter—who could tire of a diet that includes these things at their freshest best?

But if we want them locally grown, we will have to go out of our way to procure them. The local branch of Big Food, with its enormous displays of everything from everywhere, is unlikely to carry local produce. Purchasing local foods in season is more likely to require a stop at a farmer's market or the purchase of a share in a community-supported farm. This is more trouble than one-stop shopping. But it can result in better food and in strengthened relationships with the places we live, the time of year it may be, and the neighbors who work the land and so feed all of us.

GOOD COOKING

According to researchers who study these things, home cooking is in a long trend of decline. Although in the past few years more people have returned to eating dinner at home, fewer of them are cooking the meal themselves. Curbside takeout, in which items from a restaurant's regular menu are delivered to the consumer's car to be taken home to eat, is a booming business. So is the sale of prepared foods in supermarkets, where an increasing percentage of sales comes from foods already cooked and packaged to eat at home. Many households have reached a point at which they could not cook if they wanted to, as they lack such basic kitchen implements as pots and pans.

Why are so many people cooking so much less than they used to? One reason is lack of time. With increasing numbers of adults working full time outside the home, no one is home to cook. Another is the sense that with restaurant meals and prepared foods so readily available, cooking is unnecessary. "No one has to cook anymore," a newspaper food writer announced recently. And some people look on cooking as something they just don't want to be bothered with. A pizza restaurant executive describes some of his best customers as "baby boomers who would rather spend time with their grandchildren than slave away in the kitchen."

And yet there are other cultural indications that suggest that cooking is not quite as disposable as all that. Businesses are flourishing that allow customers to assemble a month's worth of frozen meals themselves from vats of prepared ingredients. Recipes are published explaining how to make cocktail hors d'oeuvres from prebaked pizza crusts. Domesticity magazines include suggestions for creating the illusion of cooking (put an onion in the oven; the house will smell as if you'd cooked all day). In each case, people are being offered the opportunity to pretend they are cooking without having actually to do so. But if cooking is irrelevant and passé, then why would anyone want to pretend to cook? Why not just buy ready-made or takeout food and be done with it?

Perhaps because on some level people realize that cooking does matter. It matters in part because of the nature of food as gift. When I am the recipient of a gift, something is required of me, namely, that I do something with it. It is no pleasure to give a gift to a purely passive recipient, someone who seems unchanged by the gift, who simply takes it, mumbles thank-you, and moves on. Even the most freely given gift of all, the gift of salvation, is given in expectation of a response, namely, faith and obedience.

Cooking can be a way of actively receiving the gift of food and actively participating in handing that gift on to others. There is something very passive about doing nothing with food but eating it. Being able to feed oneself is a significant developmental milestone, as anyone knows who has helped a baby figure out how to get that cracker from highchair tray to mouth. Being able to cook for oneself and for others is at least as significant. Particularly in a highly industrialized and urban society, in which the vast majority of people grow little or none of the food they eat, learning to cook and practicing the art of cooking can be a way of being involved with food not simply as a consumer but as a producer as well.

When we cook, we produce things to eat, of course, but we produce something else too: acts of care. I once got a message saying that one of my colleagues had fallen seriously ill and a mutual friend was assembling gifts of food to be taken to the family. I had happened to cook a pot roast the night before, and my family was looking forward to the leftovers. Under the circumstances, I decided that perhaps this colleague's family had more of a claim on the leftovers than we did. I packed up the pot roast with its carrots and gravy, some mashed potatoes, and a salad, and sent it off. A few weeks later I spoke with the colleague's wife. "When I opened that package," she said, "I cried. I thought, 'She cooked for me!'"

I didn't have the heart to tell her that I hadn't exactly cooked for her; I had just sent her our leftovers. And yet there was a sense in which I had cooked for her. Cooking is something that naturally overflows its boundaries, that leads to there being leftovers to share with someone, a pot of soup that can stretch to feed a guest or two, an extra loaf of bread to give to a neighbor. And on days when cooking feeds only those who are members of the household, it is a way to enact our gratitude for the gift of food, our pleasure in preparing it and eating it, and the mutual caring that we want to characterize our relationships as Christian people.

Cooking also fosters an engagement with the real things of real life. Too often, in our rushed and technology-saturated society, people are tempted to substitute the virtual for the actual, the imaginary for the real. Where food is concerned, we see this in the development of so-called food porn, in which sensual images of food substitute for the real thing. Increasing numbers of cookbooks full of glossy photographs are sold, but it is believed that few of them are used for cooking. As one commentator remarks, "Food photography, especially in cookbooks, has become analogous to safe sex. It's a salacious, sensual, visually tantalizing experience with no guilt or calories."

One suspects that a problem with such cookbooks is analogous to a central problem with the more traditional sort of pornography: that a steady diet of fantasy about impossible perfection dulls one's appetite for the real thing and damages one's ability to appreciate it. Fantasies about cooking may seem harmless, and perhaps in small measure they are. But reality is where our actual lives and bodies and relationships are located, and it is with real food, not fantasies about food, that those lives and bodies and relationships are nourished.

Most people have many claims on their time. Whatever daily cooking we do for our households is not likely to be fancy. But if we make realistic plans, shop for quality ingredients, and take adequate time to prepare them, we can make real food that truly satisfies. And perhaps our willing engagement with the realities of food and cooking will spill over into deeper engagement with other realities of life—in particular, the people who are members of our households and of the larger household of God.

GOOD COMPANY

When my son was a toddler, I read a child-rearing book that included a discussion of how children should be fed. The author, voicing her frustration about ways in which she felt family relationships could interfere with appropriate feeding practices, said, "Eating is not a social event! Eating is about nutrition, period."

This author meant well, but she could not have been more wrong. Food and eating are at least as much about social relationships as they are about nutrition. We will feed ourselves and one another with much more pleasure and satisfaction if we can acknowledge and embrace the ways in which food connects us with those around us rather than rejecting or ignoring such connections or regarding them as suspect or problematic.

One way in which food expresses connections between people is through the preparation and eating of foods that are traditional. Some traditional foods may be related to secular or churchly holidays like Thanksgiving or Christmas. Others may be ethnic or national—the Italian or Swedish or Korean cuisines that our immigrant forebears brought with them to a new country; the fried chicken or chili or steamed lobster that may have characterized the American regional cuisine we grew up with.

Now that ethnic and regional foods and even holiday meals are widely available in restaurants, it may seem unnecessary to preserve these traditions of cooking and eating in our own households. And yet preserving the practices of cooking and eating traditional dishes can be a way of affirming and living out the particular inheritances we receive from our forebears and then passing these on to those who come after us.

I once ordered some oxtail at my local supermarket, explaining to the butcher that I planned to make oxtail soup. "My grandmother made the most wonderful oxtail soup," the butcher said, looking wistful. A few months later I bought some rhubarb. "My grandmother makes the most wonderful rhubarb pie," sighed the checker as he rang up my purchase.

I wondered whether either of these men had ever thought to ask his grandmother to teach him to cook these dishes. If they had, perhaps one day some young person would smile and say, "My grandfather makes the most wonderful oxtail soup (or rhubarb pie)." What dishes are part of our culinary heritage? What foods express something of who we are or where our families have come from, that we can then hand on to those who come after us, whether those are people we have fed or people we have taught to cook?

Dietary preferences are another area in which individual practices can either foster or hinder connections with others. The trend in modern American culture is toward ever more individualized eating. Diets are touted as suitable for people of a particular body type or even of a particular blood type. Deciding what one will or will not eat becomes a primary means of defining one's own individuality: "I don't eat carbs," "I don't eat fat," "I don't eat red meat," "I don't eat animal products," "I don't eat cooked food."

And with every food added to the list of things one does not eat, the shorter becomes the list of people with whom one can enjoy table fellowship. Dietary practices become a means of warding off contact not only with foods that are deemed objectionable but also with people who are deemed objectionable because they eat whatever it is that the diet forbids. Like the religious reformer who considers himself too spiritually pure to worship with others, the modern American dieter often ends up too pure to eat with others.

Of course there are people whose dietary preferences or restrictions are a matter of necessity. Where this is the case, honoring those preferences or restrictions by serving and sharing acceptable foods can be a profound expression of hospitality and mutuality. But for those of us whose health permits, partaking readily of whatever is offered can be a way of affirming that eating together is at least as important as whatever it is that is eaten.

A few years ago I traveled abroad to attend an ecumenical conference at which meals were served family-style—with everyone taking portions from a common dish. One evening the flavor of the main course seemed vaguely unfamiliar. Examining the bones on my plate, I guessed that it was rabbit. I had a hard time imagining a similar scene in an American institutional dining room, where any menu would have included a choice of main course (and rabbit would not have been one of the choices).

I didn't rush home to cook a rabbit myself. But it was fine. Delicious, actually. More than that, as the eight or ten of us around that table—Europeans, Africans, Americans—ate our common meal from that common dish, we affirmed and experienced a fellowship with one another as members of the human family and of the household of God that I suspect would have been difficult to match had we chosen food to suit our individual preferences from a menu or a cafeteria line.

The simple act of eating together is perhaps the most fundamental of all the ways in which food can express and foster the community that God desires should exist among people and between humans and God. Of the four great meals that structure the biblical account of creation and redemption, three are fundamentally communal: the Passover meal, the Eucharistic meal, and the wedding supper of the Lamb. Only the first, Adam and Eve's eating of the forbidden fruit, is not obviously a common meal. On the contrary, as the story is told, first Eve ate, and then Adam, and within minutes, it seems, they were hiding from each other (behind fig leaves) and from God (behind trees).

There is a sense in which the rest of scripture can be seen as an account of God's efforts to get humans back at the table with each other and with himself. We read in Exodus of God's provision of manna in the wilderness, and elsewhere in the Old Testament of other miraculous meals, like those shared by the widow of Zarephath and the prophet Elijah. We read in the New Testament of the meals Jesus shared with his disciples, his friends, and his enemies and of the kingdom of God as a magnificent banquet to which all are invited.

All of which is good reason to see the sharing of food and of mealtime as a practice that participates in and points toward the kingdom of God. Of course people may eat alone from time to time, particularly if they live alone. Even then a prayer of thanks before the meal can make a solitary dinner one that is in a real sense shared with both God and the larger household of God, and occasional or frequent guests can expand the circle of table fellowship beyond the household itself.

For those of us who live in shared households, eating with our fellow household members is a practice that is worth fostering—perhaps not every meal, perhaps not every day, but as a general rule rather than as an exception. If we live with other people but eat by ourselves, just how deep is our common life? As Christians, we do well to eat of one loaf and drink of one cup, not just at the communion table but also at the dinner table. We are called by God to be members one of another, and one way to say that with our bodies is to sit down at the same table at the same time and break bread together. As we do this with our fellow household members and with whatever friends or strangers God may have brought to our table, we anticipate the day when we will all sit down together at God's banqueting table to eat and to give thanks together.

7

Feeding a Household

———

In the movie *Babette's Feast,* the title character is a French-woman who flees to Denmark to escape danger in her native land. She comes to the door of two Danish sisters, bearing with her a letter of introduction from a mutual friend that ends, "Babette can cook." The sisters cannot afford to pay her—indeed, they fear they cannot afford even to feed her—but they take her in, offering her refuge in exchange for her services as a cook.

And so Babette cooks. She cooks the salt cod and bread porridge that the sisters teach her to make for them. She shops with an attention to economy and quality that makes the sisters' small income go further than it did before. She distributes gifts of food to the sick and needy members of the community. And at the climax of the film, she creates a feast that terrifies the sisters in its grandeur and strangeness while simultaneously transforming and healing them and their entire community.

Babette's Feast has sometimes been interpreted as an allegory of the Eucharist in which the gifts of bread and wine communicate the transforming grace of Christ to recipients who are often as suspicious and fearful as the guests at

Babette's feast and who, like those guests, are healed and restored nonetheless. The Eucharist, of course, is the shared
meal of the household of God, and there is a sense in which
the entire film can be seen as a portrait of the range of activities involved in feeding any Christian household.

A notable feature of the cooking that Babette does is
how plain most of it is. The feast at the end is elaborate, yes,
but this has been preceded in the story by a good twenty
years in which the menu has consisted of salt fish, bread, soup,
and not much else. Perhaps this diet is more spartan than it
really has to be. One gets the sense that the sisters reject the
potential pleasures of the table with more vigor than necessary and that one of Babette's gifts to them is the careful and
tasty preparation of even these staple foods.

And yet the basic reality remains—most of the food on
the sisters' table is plain food. And so is most traditional home
cooking, in whatever place or time. Soups and stews, bread or
rice or pasta, fruits and vegetables in season, perhaps some
meat or fish or cheese—these are the things that people eat
day in and day out as elements of the regular meals that provide their regular nourishment.

In a culture such as ours, one that prizes novelty and
variety above tradition or routine, the tendency of home
cooking to produce the same old thing can seem like a strike
against it. Why eat pea soup every Thursday night, the way
your immigrant grandparents did, when you can choose from
dozens of frozen entrées or ready-made dishes at your local
supermarket?

The reality is, though, that the apparent variety of the
frozen-food case masks the soy-and-corn monotony of
global agribusiness that underlies it. And shopping the
frozen-food aisle becomes a routine unto itself as people

scan the shelves searching for a little box they can open for dinner. Perhaps it might be better, at least some of the time, to drop by the farm stand for some of whatever is in season, pull a package of noodles down from the cupboard, and have the food on the table be something that we ourselves have made, some basic dish that we know well and that reflects the traditions we have inherited and the places and times in which we live.

Another aspect of Babette's work as a cook is how busy she is. She spends as much time procuring her ingredients as she does cooking them and as much time again serving the prepared food to the sisters or taking it around to needy members of the community. Feeding a household and its neighbors and guests is a big job, in other words, one that ebbs and flows with times and days and seasons but that continues from day to day and from year to year.

It is this never-ending quality to the job of feeding a household that can make it seem like such a burden. There never comes a day when no one has to think about what is for breakfast or lunch or dinner because every day people are going to be hungry and will need to be fed. At the same time, it is precisely this ongoing need that makes feeding a household akin to the providential work of God. When we pray, "Give us this day our daily bread," we are asking and trusting God to do exactly what we are called to do for one another: to feed one another, every day, readily and without complaint.

Embracing—rather than resisting—the daily necessity of feeding a household can be a way of embracing the privilege of participating with God in this aspect of providential care. Feeding a household is not an achievement that, once accomplished, can be checked off and set aside to make room for other pursuits. Feeding a household is an act of faithfulness, one that requires daily energy and attention and whose pleasures and rewards are experienced in the course of that faithfulness rather than only at the end.

At the end of *Babette's Feast,* of course, is the feast itself— and this suggests a third characteristic of the work of feeding a household. Most meals are everyday meals, but some meals are—and should be—feasts. Most of us will never prepare a feast as magnificent as Babette's, for the simple reason that most of us cannot cook as well as Babette (who, it turns out, was a great chef in France before her exile). But our households will always have reasons to celebrate, from family occasions like birthdays or weddings to great church holidays like Christmas and Easter.

Special meals and special foods recur throughout Christian scripture and tradition as appropriate, even necessary, ways of celebrating and rejoicing in the good gifts of God. From the feasts celebrating the wedding at Cana and the return of the prodigal son, to the traditional holiday foods that have developed in all Christian cultures, we find the people of God preparing and sharing meals that express their joy in God's present grace and their hope in his future and ultimate faithfulness.

A household feast might be as elaborate as a dinner with many courses served on fine china to a table full of invited guests or as simple as a birthday child's favorite dish followed by cupcakes with candles stuck in them. A meal is a feast not because any particular amount of money has been spent or any particular level of sumptuousness achieved, but because time and care has been taken to make this meal an event that all around the table can celebrate together, taking pleasure in the food, the company, the occasion—all of which, in their own way, are foretastes of the kingdom of God.

PLANNING

Even those who attend Christian worship every week may not realize how much thought has gone into putting together a worship service. "A few prayers, a few hymns, a sermon," they think. "How hard can it be?" In fact, the church's worship is the result of hours of planning—centuries, even, considering the development of church music and liturgy over time. Many a new minister, musician, or worship committee member, surrounded by biblical texts, hymnbooks, creeds, and calendars, has learned that what seemed simple from the pew is actually quite complex. And so he or she turns to the lectionary (a calendar of Bible readings), to a service book, or to more experienced worship leaders for help in planning meaningful worship for others.

Planning meals is not so different from planning worship. There are the clock and the calendar to consider: What time of day will the meal be? What day of the week? What season of the year? There is the audience to consider: Who are we feeding? Adults? Children? Guests? Does anyone have particular dietary needs or preferences? And then there are the limits of our schedules and of our purses: Do we have a lot of time to cook or only a little? Do we have a lot of money to spend or only a little?

Like worship planning, meal planning is a skill that is honed by experience; the longer you have been at it, the more instinctive becomes your approach to it, until you are able to make many of the decisions involved without consciously thinking about it. But until those instincts have been formed, there is a lot of thought required and a lot of need for consulting the culinary equivalents of lectionaries and service books (that is, cookbooks) and especially other people—people who are also busy in the kitchen and whose experience may prove helpful to our own practice.

Among the helpful culinary advisers I have encountered is Robert Farrar Capon, an Episcopal priest who wrote several books about cooking. In one of them, *The Supper of the Lamb,* Capon offers a couple of pieces of advice that are particularly relevant where meal planning is concerned. The first word has to do with everyday cooking, what Capon calls "ferial cuisine," as opposed to special-occasion, feast-day cooking. As Capon sees it, the principal rule of ferial cuisine is "Never serve anybody a whole anything."

Everyday food, in other words, is not about steaks and chops and boneless breasts of chicken. Everyday food is about meatloaf and casseroles, pots of pasta and loaves of bread. It is about dishes that can take a bit of leftover something and stretch it to feed the household, like the end of Sunday's pork roast that becomes a dish of fried rice. It is about dishes that are made not just for tonight but for several nights, like the pot of soup whose leftovers go into the refrigerator or freezer, to emerge later in the week or month on an evening when there is no time or desire to cook.

Even if we choose not to follow the letter of Capon's advice (why not serve salmon steaks on a weeknight once in a while, after all?), there is a lot of wisdom in its spirit. Everyday food is about moderation. It is about moderation of expense, in that "whole things" (like steaks or chops) are expensive, and rare is the household whose food budget allows such things on a nightly basis. And it is about moderation of consumption. It is about eating half of a dish tonight so as to have the other half left for tomorrow, or eating lightly this evening because tomorrow evening there

will be company and thus a larger meal or something special for dessert.

And it is about moderation of effort. Perhaps the analogy to worship can be helpful here too. Religious communities can find themselves inclined to express their
seriousness about worship by making their worship services
longer and longer and more and more elaborate until their
common life threatens to collapse under the weight of liturgical exercises that absorb every bit of the community's
energy. Taking the work of feeding a household seriously
could conceivably end up like this, with people feeling that
they are doing it right only if they are spending hours shopping and cooking every day and ending up with no time to
do anything else.

On the other hand, there can be those who doubt
whether worship is really a good use of one's time and who
are tempted to slight it in favor of other seemingly more
productive activities. The culinary equivalent of this inclination seems to me to be the more common temptation in our
day, as the advertising industry bombards us with exhorta-
tions to purchase this or that frozen or microwavable item so
that we will have more time for other—presumably more
important—things. Moderation in everyday cooking may for
some of us mean taking more time for it, not only time to
cook and eat but time to plan and time to shop, so that we
can put a tasty, simple meal on the table.

Capon's other helpful word of advice has to do with
considering the preferences of one's audience. Capon, a
father of six, puts it in terms of children: "Feed your children,
of course, but cook for yourself." By this he does not mean
that you should cook multiple meals, one for each of the
children and one for yourself. He means that you should plan

meals that accommodate differences of taste but not allow those differences to dictate everything that goes on in—or comes out of—your kitchen.

Market research firms have found that increasing numbers of households do produce customized meals for their individual members. The number of main dishes on family tables is increasing, even as the total number of dishes declines. The intention appears to be to keep peace among household members with mutually incompatible preferences, but the result is exhaustion and irritation for the cook, along with—perhaps more important—a loss of the table fellowship that comes when meals are truly shared rather than simply eaten in the general proximity of other people.

But it is true that individual tastes and preferences do vary. Is there a way to allow for these real differences in taste while also enjoying the real community engendered by eating together around a common table? In the sixth century, Saint Benedict answered this question by specifying that there should always be two dishes served at dinner so that anyone who could not or did not want to eat one dish could serve himself from the other. Modern Benedictine communities sometimes adapt this rule by serving two main dishes at each evening meal, in addition to whatever starch and vegetable side dishes are offered.

An ordinary household might serve only one main dish, accompanied by side dishes that will be generally liked even if the main dish is not. There is nothing wrong with children filling up on bread or fruit if they prefer that to tuna casserole, particularly if the bread and fruit are on the table to begin with. That way, they are not rejecting dinner; they are simply choosing from what is offered.

COOKING

I have never much liked microwave ovens. They come in very handy for a few particular limited uses—melting butter, thawing frozen soup, reheating leftovers. But there is something very alienating about putting food in a box, pushing a button, and retrieving it a few minutes or seconds later in the hope that it is now a better temperature. Real cooking, it seems to me, happens on a stove or in an oven, where dishes can be stirred and aromas can escape and the cooking process is accessible and invites, even requires, interaction with the cook.

Not everyone experiences this as a good thing. I once cooked a special dish for a group of people who ate it up with expressions of delight while simultaneously exclaiming about how they had watched their own mothers make this dish and had resolved never to go to that kind of trouble themselves. I puzzled for years over that one—all these lovely, kind people who thought the dish was so delicious and who were so firmly convinced that it would be a waste of time to cook it that they thought it would be a good idea to inform me, the cook, of this.

I could only conclude that in a world filled with push-button "convenience," the tactile, interactive nature of cooking can seem like a problem to be overcome rather than an opportunity to be engaged. This seems to be the assumption of authors of books like one called *Semi-Homemade Cooking*, who tout the use of packaged ingredients and disposable dishes on the grounds that these items "provide quick preparation and cleanup—you'll minimize your work while maximizing your leisure time."

How different this is from Julia Child, who in an episode of her classic television show *The French Chef* describes French onion soup as "fun to make and delicious to eat." You can bet that Julia is not making her onion soup in a disposable pot from a packaged mix in order to minimize her work and maximize her leisure. On the contrary: Julia is slicing real onions into a real pot, and precisely because she enjoys the making and enjoys the eating, she doesn't need "leisure," at least not the convenience-food variety.

It seems to me that Julia Child's attitude toward onion soup expresses something akin to the properly Christian delight in created things that ought to characterize our relationship to food and cooking. It is glorious that there are such things as onions and even more glorious that people have figured out how to make things like French onion soup out of them. One of the ways that we can express our delight in God's good gifts is through a wholehearted willingness to cook and eat real food made with real ingredients—like onions.

Good tools are a part of the cook's delight. To a cook with a dull knife in hand, an onion can seem like the most intractable of enemies. To a cook with a sharp knife, the onion yields rings, slivers, dice, their crisp edges and regular shape a foreshadowing of the pleasure yet to come with the completed dish. Other tools bring their own particular pleasures—the ricer that makes perfectly smooth and fluffy mashed potatoes, the flat whisk that helps blend every bit of pan dripping into the gravy, the cherry pitter that rhythmically pops the pits out of that mound of sour cherries en route to becoming a pie.

How much of this equipment is truly necessary? I would definitely take the knife with me to a desert island; for the rest of it, it would depend on how long I had to pack. It is certainly true that cooking—like so many other aspects of the Christian life—is much more about what you do with the resources at your disposal than it is about what those resources are. Many is the person with limited funds or limited space or both who has turned out pot after pot of delicious soup or stew with little more to hand than a knife, a pot, and a hot plate. We might wish to have bigger or better-equipped kitchens than in fact we do, but what matters is the faithful production of dinner (and lunch and breakfast) in the kitchens we do have.

The best kitchen tools, of course, are ones that are genuinely suited to the task. These days, the fantasy of cooking is more visibly popular than cooking itself is, and a great deal of the cookware that is for sale is more about fantasies of gleaming kitchens full of expensive, oversize equipment than it is about the realities of cupboard space and daily use. The result is that some of the best (meaning the most truly useful) kitchen equipment is to be found in thrift shops and the junky sort of antique stores that carry inexpensive bits and pieces from decades ago, when lots of people cooked and the assumption was that you needed good serviceable cookware that didn't cost a fortune or take up a lot of room.

The other advantage of old cookware is that it brings the lives and stories of other people into your kitchen. I went to an estate sale once and found an aluminum colander that was similar to but larger and sturdier than the one I'd had for years and that had recently lost one of its legs. Now as I use that colander I occasionally reflect on the woman who first owned it. I imagine she must have been a good cook, to have had so nice a colander and to have given it as much wear as it shows. I have other old things that I inherited from my grandmother—a candy thermometer, a stainless-steel spoon with a wooden handle, a set of rectangular canisters—each of which ties my work as a cook to the work of generations of cooks before me.

A time when many people feel both pressure and desire to cook and to cook well is the "holiday season," namely Thanksgiving and Christmas. These are an odd pair of holidays, the first unrelated to the Christian calendar and yet invested with all kinds of quasi-religious sentimentality, the second ostensibly Christian and yet a vehicle for the crassest commercialism and most frantic hyperactivity imaginable. But both give a central place to food in that both are times when most of us would like to see our families and others seated around a table laden with dishes that we have had a hand in preparing.

It might be helpful at the outset to cut both holidays down to size. Thanksgiving is a nice chance to eat a turkey and get together with family and friends or strangers; Christmas is a bona fide Christian feast day with a lot of pleasant if extraneous traditions associated with it—cookies, cards, trees, presents. That said, times like these can be occasions on which the cook comes into his or her own, when disciplines and skills developed throughout the course of the year have a chance to shine in the preparation of a special meal.

In this sense, holiday cooking is for the household cook as running a race is for an athlete—an occasional, strenuously exhilarating event, in contrast to the kind of regular exercise that takes place from day to day. In *Babette's Feast,* the analogy is to a musician who practices for days and years and then gives a beautiful performance that showcases her artistry—not so much for the purpose of dazzling her audience (although that does happen) as for the intrinsic, deeply rooted pleasure that a great performance gives to the artist herself and for the glory that this reflects on the Author and Giver of that artistry, God himself.

Not everyone likes to cook or is equally good at cooking. In a world in which there are so many different things to like and to be good at, that is not surprising. Not everyone is the same, and that is part of the glory of creation. But the need to eat and the opportunity to enjoy the pleasures of the table are universal, and it is these needs and opportunities that the art of cooking serves.

DINING

The point of cooking is to feed people, and so no meal is truly finished until it has been eaten. The food exists for the sake of the meal, and those who eat are just as important participants as those who cook. Sitting down at the table is as significant an act as setting the food on the table; eating with appreciation is as much an art as preparing food with generosity and care.

One would think that a culture of abundance like the one we inhabit would engender gratitude and delight in the recipients of its bounty. Unfortunately, the opposite is too often the case, as abundance becomes overabundance and potentially healthy appetites become jaded by the seemingly infinite amounts and variety of foods available. The result is that too many diners sit down at the table expecting not simply to be fed but to be impressed or placated or otherwise cajoled into eating. Advertising campaigns certainly operate on this assumption; one ad, for a national brand of canned soup, features a child who grins and munches something identified as "2-Step Beefy Taco Joes" as her parents look anxiously on. The caption reads, "Sometimes all it takes is 2 steps to wow the world's most important food critic."

If this is what cooking for a household amounts to—pacifying tyrannical children with brand-name processed food—then it is no wonder that fewer and fewer people want anything to do with it. Cooking is enjoyable if, and only if, the cook has a reasonable expectation that the people being cooked for will eat with appreciation and enjoyment. This is an art that can be cultivated. A pastor I know relates a story about a child who had been taught always to compliment the cook. One day as this child was eating his lunch he remarked, "Mom, this hot dog is delicious! I know you didn't make it yourself, but it is just the right temperature!"

In Christian scripture, there are moral implications to accepting or rejecting meals and invitations to meals. Jesus tells a sobering parable about guests who were invited to a marriage feast for a king's son but wouldn't come (Matthew 22). The king was not at all pleased and found other people to take the places around his table. As we practice the discipline of receiving thankfully the food that is offered to us on our own tables, and as we teach our children to do the same, we may become better able to respond to God with pleasure and gratitude as he invites us to his table.

The table itself is a powerful symbol of fellowship among humans and between humans and God. Even in the presence of enemies, says the psalmist, God prepares a table before us and fills our cup to overflowing (Psalm 23). Elsewhere in the Old Testament (Exodus 25:23–30; 1 Kings 7:48) we read of the tabernacle and of the temple, both of which served as dwelling places for God with his people and both of which included prominently among their furnishings a sumptuously beautiful golden table furnished with golden utensils and bearing on it the "bread of the Presence" that symbolized God's own presence with his people.

In the New Testament it is Jesus himself who is present among human beings as the bread of life. It is Jesus who sits at table—with his disciples, with tax collectors and sinners, with Pharisees—and teaches them about the kingdom of God in stories that as often as not include meals and tables. Jesus presided at table over a meal with his disciples on the night he was betrayed, and after his resurrection he sat again at table with some of those disciples. As the evangelist Luke tells the story, Jesus had spent the entire afternoon explaining the scriptures to his companions, but not until they broke bread together did they recognize him (Luke 24:30–31). Their fellowship around the table was revelatory in a way that teaching alone had not been.

Tables have continued to occupy central physical and liturgical space in the life of the church. Early Christians celebrated their love feasts on tables set over the graves of the martyrs. These tables gave rise in later Catholic tradition to the altars on which the sacrament of the Mass was celebrated and in Protestant practice to tables at which the Lord's Supper was observed.

Christian households might do well to give a similarly central place to the tables at which they eat their common meals. A meal can be eaten without a table, to be sure. Presumably there were no tables when Jesus fed the crowds on the hillside. But most meals are properly eaten at a table, preferably one that has been thoughtfully set to be both beautiful and ceremonial, like the tables of the tabernacle and the temple.

This does not mean we all need to go out and have our dining tables gold-plated or even that we need to use the good china every day or acquire some if we haven't got any.

On the other hand, if we do have good china, why not use it? And even very ordinary dishes can be used to set an attractive table if we take the time to set a place for each person, to arrange the utensils neatly next to the plates, to put out glasses for water or for wine, and to put the food on the table in serving dishes rather than the pots and pans it was cooked in. Whatever the occasion, setting the table can serve to set the meal itself apart from the other activities that fill the day and to create a space in which time and attention can be devoted to receiving together the gifts of food and of fellowship with whoever else may be gathered around the table.

The custom of saying table grace is another means of setting mealtime apart from the rest of the day, and of acknowledging God as the source of all good gifts and of this food and this fellowship in particular. Table graces may vary from short blessings said or sung from memory to longer or shorter extemporaneous prayers said by one or more members of the household. Cooks generally prefer shorter graces so that the food doesn't get cold. This is, after all, a mealtime prayer!

Having cooked the meal and assembled the family, set the table, and said our prayer, the temptation is to want every particular meal to repay all that effort by being memorable in some obvious way, a kind of Norman Rockwell snapshot of Christian community life. But the fact is that most meals are not particularly memorable, and that is probably just as well. Who would wish to keep perpetually in mind this rather ordinary menu, that lapse in the children's table manners, this conversation consisting of the less than fascinating details of a less than fascinating day?

But meals need not be individually memorable to be nourishing. Many of a congregation's individual celebrations of the Lord's Supper may be largely indistinguishable from one another, and yet the sustained practice of sharing to-gether at the Lord's table is one of the ways the household of God is nourished and built up together over time. So too a Christian household's shared meals may include many occa-sions that are rather routine, and that is the point. It is rou-tines like these from which the fabric of our common life is woven as household members gather around the table to eat meals that one or several of us have prepared.

CLEANING UP

Kathleen Norris tells a story about attending a Catholic Mass for the first time and being fascinated by the busyness of the priest as he puttered about the altar after the Eucharist, put-ting things in neat piles, organizing the plates that had held the wafers, rinsing and wiping the chalice. Suddenly it dawned on her: he is washing the dishes!

It seemed delightfully incongruous to her. What could be more everyday than washing dishes? And yet this everyday activity was taking place in sacred space, suggesting that per-haps the sacred and the mundane are not so separate after all, that perhaps they touch each other at more points than we sometimes imagine.

The kitchen sink is not, perhaps, the first place that we might think of as being one of those joining points of earth and heaven. Dishwashing itself, though, is a kind of liminal task; it takes place at the edges of things, as we finish one meal and set the stage for another, as we wash dirty pots and pans and glasses and plates and put them away clean for their next use.

Tasks that exist at the margins of other things have the potential to frame those other things in ways that enhance them or detract from them. The way in which we clean up after a meal will inevitably affect how we cook and how we eat, and also how our cooking and eating nourish our lives both individually and together. And as we weave dishwashing into our domestic liturgies, we may find that it takes on a sort of humble significance of its own, even as the priest's dishwashing occupies its own particular place in the Eucharistic liturgy.

Washing dishes is a task that begins before the meal itself as we busy ourselves with preparation and cooking. Beginning cooks sometimes imagine that first you cook and later you clean up. Not a few parents have entered the kitchen with dismay after a child's efforts at cooking dinner. The meal itself may have turned out fine, but there are pots and utensils and spilled bits of this and that everywhere because the apprentice cook has whirled through the kitchen with no thought for making washing up a part of the process.

Experienced cooks clean as they go, scraping dishes and utensils and stacking them in the sink and taking a moment here or there to wash a pot and put it in the dish rack to drain. There is a place for planning your menu and your methods to dirty as few dishes as possible (particularly if you don't have very many dishes to begin with), but kitchen utensils are tools, and tools are meant to be used—and washed and put away to be used again.

That tools are meant to be used would seem to go without saying, but this is another point at which contemporary culture blares a contradictory message. Domesticity magazines are filled with articles about just what expensive brands of cookware are the best, side by side with more articles about how to avoid dirtying any of it by using disposable dishes, all surrounded by ads for packaged foods pitched as means for freeing people from the need to cook—or clean up—at all.

But a kitchen is meant to be dynamic rather than static; you equip a kitchen so you can work in it, not so you can look at it or bypass it on the way to the microwave. This is why a kitchen that is truly equipped for cooking always has a dish drainer in it. Actually, I have known a few good cooks who have no dish drainer. I don't know what they do without one. If after you use a knife you put it in the dishwasher, it is not clean and ready to be used the next time you need it. The place for used kitchen utensils is in the sink, ready to be washed, or in the dish drainer, ready to be used again or put away.

Good knives—and good dishes and good pots and pans—shouldn't go in the dishwasher at all. For this reason it can be just as well not to have a dishwasher. People who have dishwashers are forever not using the good knives or the good dishes because they can't go in the dishwasher. My house has neither a dishwasher nor space for a dishwasher, and while it could come in mighty handy to have either (the dishwasher or space for one), I do appreciate the freedom that not having a dishwasher gives me to use whatever dishes I like, without any concern that using the nicer ones is somehow going to make more work.

Before the dishes can be washed, the table must be cleared, preferably after everyone has finished eating. While there may be good reason to allow children to leave the table before everyone is done, I have never cared for the custom of teaching them to clear their places when they do so. It disrupts the rhythm of the meal to have the clearing away begun before the meal is finished; those who linger over their plates are left eating at a half-set table, wondering whether someone is about to snatch away their plates too.

Allowing a child to clear his or her place when excused from the table also fosters the impression that once the place is cleared, the child's responsibilities have been fulfilled and the child needn't bother about the rest of the things on the table or in the kitchen. But a meal is a collective enterprise, and so is cleaning up. Some diners may well want or need to be excused before everyone else has finished eating, and that is fine. But bring one or all of them back when the meal is finished to take a turn in clearing away and washing up for everyone as a part of the shared privilege and responsibility of eating together.

There is a peaceful kind of wrapping up involved in washing dishes. You are putting the kitchen to bed, putting everything back where it goes so it will be ready next time. This can be a pleasant task to do alone, after the hubbub of mealtime. It can also be a pleasant task to share, as the occupation of washing and drying and putting away creates a setting in which companionable conversation can flourish.

This opportunity for combining practical labor and companionable conversation is near the center of what it means to make a household together. A friend of mine tells a story about her college-age daughter, who was sharing an apartment with two classmates. On visits to the apartment, my friend was struck by what a wreck the place always seemed to be. Dirty dishes, in particular, seemed to cover every surface. When she asked why, her daughter airily replied, "Oh, we got to talking. Talking is important; dishes aren't." My friend reported that she had thought (but not said), "But can't you talk while you do the dishes?"

Indeed, this is one of the differences between simply living together and being members of a shared household. In a shared household, talking and dishes are equally important.

This does not mean that they must always be done simultaneously. There are times when it is important to talk first and do dishes after. But there are other times—and these come more often, in my experience—when work, particularly routine work like dishes, and conversation coexist happily and even enhance each other. At such times domestic chores provide a context for conversation in which there is a kind of added ease that allows for unhurried reflection, for greater frankness, for whatever the moment turns out to be ripe for.

That several college-age young people should see their status as roommates as an opportunity for friendship rather than for making a home together is perhaps not surprising, even if regrettable. But it is all too easy even for spouses or for parents and children to see things like dishwashing as distractions from relationship or from leisure and to put them off or rush through them in order to get on to seemingly more important things. But dishes, along with other kinds of domestic work, can be opportunities to share together in the work of making a peaceable and pleasant home, and in the process to enjoy the kind of shared time and conversation that turn out to build relationships and nourish the soul.

The Well-Kept House

The longing for home is a deeply ingrained, authentically human yearning. We long for home because we were created for home. We are created to live in peaceable communion with our surroundings and with our fellow human beings, working together to help the land yield its produce, sharing together around the table that the Lord sets before us, celebrating the goodness of creation and community.

Yet we are often frustrated in our longing for home. As a sad consequence of human sin, such things as comfortable shelter, adequate clothing, and regular meals are too often in short supply. The work required to produce them is too often experienced as exhausting or frustrating. Relationships within the household may be anything but peaceful. The loveliness and refreshment of humans' first God-given home can seem dim beyond recall.

In this situation, how appropriate it is that God's promise of redemption so often takes the form of a welcome home. Indeed, homecoming is a central image throughout the Bible. God called Abraham out of his native country not to make him permanently homeless but to give him a new home in the Promised Land. And as the writer of the letter to the Hebrews points out, even that home in the Promised

Land was like a mere tent compared with the ultimate home planned by God for his people, "the city which has foundations, whose builder and maker is God" (Hebrews 11:10).

No earthly home will ever take the place of that heavenly home to which all of the members of the household of God have looked forward in faith. And yet earthly homes really do—or can—participate in God's redemptive promise of home. Early Christians were vitally concerned for relationships and conduct within the home, to the point that a well-managed household was thought to be a sign of fitness for church office (1 Timothy 3:5).

The authors of scripture do not tell us in great detail what they think is involved in managing a household well, but they do tell us one of the characteristics of such a household. A good household is a hospitable household. Encouragement toward hospitality abounds in scripture: not only church leaders but the entire Christian community is to be hospitable, both to neighbors within the community of faith (Romans 12:13; 1 Peter 4:9) and even to strangers, "for thereby some have entertained angels unawares" (Hebrews 13:2).

This happened to Abraham and Sarah. They offered a meal to three strangers who appeared at their door one day, and after dinner the strangers delivered God's promise that Abraham and Sarah, in their old age, would have a son (Genesis 18:1–15). And we read in the New Testament of many instances in which believers opened their homes to one another, whether on a regular basis for congregational worship or for teaching and evangelism. The closing image of the book of Acts (28:30) is that of Paul in Rome, opening his home to all who came to him.

This is a very different picture from the one familiar in modern American culture. Today, it is easy to reduce "hospitality" to a nice extra (the dinner party to which you invite

family or friends on a night when no one has anything else
to do) or a component of a business school curriculum (the
hospitality industry, meaning hotels and restaurants, whose
members, if you have money, will sell you a room or a meal).
Hospitality does not necessarily have any moral resonance; it
is just something you do or don't do.

But in the culture of ancient Israel, out of which the
church was born, hospitality was among the moral foundation stones of society. Israel was a wandering stranger, and
God took her in, and fed her and clothed her and housed
her; and in response, Israel was to care for the alien and
stranger in her midst. Christians in their turn saw hospitality
as a basic way in which members of the Christian community could emulate and hand on the welcome they had received from God.

Hospitality, understood in this way, has less to do with
dinner parties than it has to do with feeding hungry people
who come to your door or who sit down at your table. It has
less to do with beautifully appointed guest rooms complete
with terrycloth robes and brand-new bars of soap than it has
to do with providing tired people with a clean and comfortable place to sleep. It has to do, in other words, with basic
provisions for basic needs—the very needs that the disciplines
involved in keeping house exist to serve.

How might we keep house, if by "keeping house" we
mean creating a home that is hospitable, both to those who
are members of the household and to those who are neighbors, guests, or strangers? To begin with, I think we will realize that elaborate, spotless perfection is really not the point.
The point is the continual re-creation of welcome and nurturance, not in some theoretical or disembodied sense but in
simple, practical provision for the needs of the body: food,
clothing, a place to sit, a place to sleep.

Ironically, perhaps (given what is often called the materialism of modern society), these basic material needs are too often met with neglect (no one makes any effort to provide clean clothes or meals) or resentment (whoever is providing the clean clothes and meals sees that work, and is encouraged by others to see it, as "drudgery"). The result is that these needs become something to indulge in fits of commercialized excess ("treating oneself" to a day at a spa or a weekend at a hotel, for example) rather than through happy daily routines of baths and meals and clean sheets.

And between bouts of indulgence (or overindulgence), we stave off longings for things that might fulfill these material needs. We view them with suspicion and fear, referring to good food, for example, as "sinfully delicious." Or we experience them only by proxy, through magazine photo spreads of sensual, quasi-pornographic pictures of food or bedding or clothes that are just to be looked at, not actually eaten or slept in or worn.

How much better it would be if we were to respond to the needs of the body not with resentment or denial or suspicion but with humility and compassion and thanksgiving! How much more hospitable it would be if our homes were routinely to be places filled with satisfying meals, with shirts warm from the dryer, with smoothly made beds—not because we are trying to win the housekeeping prize but because these are good and pleasant ways to care for one another and for ourselves!

If housekeeping is to be an expression of hospitality, it is not necessary for the house to be grand or for the cooking or cleaning or laundry to achieve some arbitrary standard of "excellence." What is required is that the members of the household contribute in whatever ways are possible and appropriate to making the home a place where household members and others can be modestly and reliably fed and clothed and housed. No one needs to be the diva of domesticity or the queen (or king) of clean. What we need is to do the best we can with what we have.

The folktales of western Europe—a culture profoundly shaped by Christian ideas and ideals—are full of stories about people who have much and will not share versus people who have little but do share. In the tale of the golden goose, three brothers encounter in turn a little man who asks them for food and drink. The first two brothers refuse to share their soft bread and wine. The third brother, who has only a dry crust and water, shares cheerfully. It is the third brother to whom the little man discloses the secret of the golden goose. He did not have anything special to share but he was blessed because he was willing to share what he had. Keeping our houses as best we can may turn out to be similarly blessed, not because our housekeeping is "perfect" but because it is a gift freely given.

ROUTINES

A few years ago I attended a performance of the National Acrobats of Taiwan. One member of the troupe was a juggler who began by tossing one ball in the air, then two, then three, then four. Then he began adding more balls—five, six, seven. Every time he increased the number of balls, the length of time he could keep them all in the air became shorter and shorter, and the number of dropped balls became greater and greater. Finally he added an eighth ball, and for a few shining seconds all eight went whirling through the air. Then, predictably, all the balls came crashing down and rolled into various dark corners of the stage, and the juggler took his bow and ran off.

For too many of us, our housekeeping practices resemble that Taiwanese juggler trying to keep eight balls in the air. We have ideas about what we want to be doing, or think we ought to be doing, that are simply overambitious. And it is easy to be overambitious because there is always something more that you could be doing. But every time we add something more, the harder it gets to keep it all going, and the more imminent and inevitable becomes the moment at which it will all come crashing down.

Unlike juggling, keeping house is not a performance that can end when it gets too complicated. Keeping house needs to continue from one day to the next, from one year to the next, if our own and others' needs for meals and clothes and welcome and rest are to be met. Realistic, sustainable routines are essential if we are to approach this work in ways that are satisfying and pleasant to ourselves and to others. It is routines like these that are at the heart of the litany of everyday life.

Housekeeping routines are akin to the sacred routines that shape the corporate life of the church. The church's routines are characterized by a rhythm of overlapping cycles corresponding to days and weeks and years. The day begins with matins (early morning prayer) and ends with vespers (evening prayer). Weeks run from Sunday to Saturday. The year begins with Advent and ends with the long season called Ordinary Time.

Sustainable household routines also include daily and weekly and yearly cycles of activity. A daily household routine may begin with fixing breakfast and making beds; perhaps it will end with doing dinner dishes and tidying up. The days of the week may provide opportunities for different tasks—a day to do laundry, a day to shop for groceries, an evening when the whole family cleans together—or opportunities for different household members to take turns at cooking or washing up. Seasonal or yearly routines may involve jobs that need only to be done occasionally—washing windows, putting away out-of-season clothing, planning and cooking holiday meals. Or they may involve a change in how daily or weekly jobs are done—hanging laundry out in the summertime rather than drying it in the dryer, adapting menus for spring or summer, fall or winter.

Inevitably, some days and seasons will be busier than others, even as sacred liturgies vary in their length and complexity according to the time of the day and week and year. But if we have some sense of what needs to be done daily and what can be done less frequently, it is much more likely that we will be able to accomplish the day's or the week's work in a way that is centered and focused rather than pervaded with an anxious or guilty sense that we really should be doing more or other than what we are in fact doing.

This points to another similarity between domestic and sacred liturgies. Neither one ever includes everything all at the same time. We sing Christmas hymns at Christmastime and Easter hymns at Eastertime. The church has over the centuries thought of certain psalms as particularly appropriate for evening or for morning. But no worship service ever includes the whole hymnal or the entire psalter all at the same time.

The domestic liturgies that comprise housekeeping also follow patterns shaped by specific times and seasons. It is not possible to do everything, all at the same time, because there is simply too much to it. Even if you are starting from behind, with a seriously disordered house or nonexistent routines, you cannot begin by doing everything right now. What you can do is begin with one day's work, or one hour's work: a meal prepared, a room tidied, a closet organized. The day's own work is sufficient for it; tomorrow will bring its own opportunities.

At the same time, however, every day does have its own work. Members of religious communities do not save all of their praying for Sunday; they pray at intervals throughout the day, allowing work and prayer thus to intertwine in their daily experience. So it is with the domestic liturgies of house-keeping. When small jobs are woven into the fabric of daily life—a floor swept here, a wastebasket emptied there, a bed made soon after its occupant has gotten out of it—then the work of making a home and the pleasure of living in a home are intertwined, rather than being experienced as separate from—or worse, opposed to—each other.

A third similarity between sacred and domestic litur-gies is that it takes time to learn to perform them with famil-iarity and ease. The British author C. S. Lewis occasionally complained about the tendency of prayer book editors con-stantly to "update" the words of the liturgy. He didn't care what particular form the liturgy actually took, he said; all he wanted was that they choose a form and then leave it alone. His point was not that liturgy should never change. His point was that if he was constantly unsure what to do and say next, it made it very difficult to enter into prayer with concentration and serenity and an openness to grace.

The routines of housekeeping have the potential to be similarly disorienting. If we are unfamiliar with the myriad tasks and subtasks involved in planning menus and cooking meals or in picking up and cleaning a house, we may feel just as confused as the Baptist who has stumbled into an Anglican church and is frantically searching for the right page in the prayer book while trying—and failing—to sit, stand, and kneel at the right times.

If the Baptist perseveres, he or she will certainly figure it out. And if we persevere in our domestic liturgies, we will figure them out too. There is no substitute for simply entering into the tasks involved in making a home and seeing what works for us and for our households and what does not. The work itself will shape us as we discover what it requires of us and what rewards it returns.

EMERGENCIES

Routines are obviously a good thing on routine days—days when nothing out of the ordinary happens, when no circumstances arise that make it difficult to go through with things as planned. But what about when such circumstances do arise? Life is unpredictable, after all. A friend was once describing her household arrangements, which included jobs outside the home for both her and her husband, school and activities for their two children, plus housework and all the other busyness of life. "It works out," she said, "as long as nobody gets sick."

But what about when somebody does get sick? What about when the washing machine breaks and someone has to stay home to wait for the repair person to come and fix it? What about when the day has been busy and the person who was going to stop by the grocery store on his or her way home has been unable to do so? What about when it has been raining all day and the children have been running in and out of the house and the floor is covered with mud?

And what about longer-term "emergencies," things that make keeping house more difficult not just for a day but for weeks or months or years? Babies are almost always emergencies in this sense—it is hard to get out to the grocery store when you have an infant in your house. And a chronically ill or disabled or elderly family member is bound to be a kind of long-term housekeeping emergency, involving special meals, extra laundry, and less time in which to do all manner of other things.

The first thing to remember concerning emergencies, whether serious or trivial, is that this is the stuff of which human life is made. Things do not go as planned; they always take more time than it seems they should; they have to be done twice when it seems that once should be enough. And the more complex or difficult the circumstances, the greater becomes the need for the kind of basic nurturance that housekeeping seeks to provide. People need dinner even on good days, and on bad days they need it even more.

A truly human life is one that is lived not only in life's strengths but in its weaknesses as well. A well-kept house is thus a house in which it is safe to be weak, because the members of the household take care of one another. And in a more everyday way, it is a house in which it is safe to be hungry (there is food in the cupboard), safe to be tired (there are places to sit and places to sleep), safe to need clean socks (there are some in the drawer, and if they all happen to be in the hamper, someone will put in a load of wash soon).

Efficiency can be the enemy of hospitable housekeeping, especially in the face of small or large emergencies. All too often, efficiency is just another name for being spread too thin. A few years ago there were massive cascading power failures all over the eastern United States that were eventually attributed in part to design features meant to make the distribution of power as efficient as possible. It turned out that because all parts of the system were working at maximum efficiency all of the time, the system as a whole had no way to adjust to problems, and small-scale disruptions rapidly became large-scale catastrophes.

Maximum efficiency in housekeeping routines can have the same effect. If we are working as fast as we can, all the time, there is no way to adjust to the inevitable disruptions. Moreover, maximum efficiency easily turns into no rest for the weary. You are never done because the plan is never to be done; the plan is to be working at something or other, full speed ahead, all the time. And maximum efficiency tends implicitly to devalue the work itself or to reflect its devaluation by others. You are working as fast as possible and doing as little as possible—why? Perhaps because you are inclined to think the work has no intrinsic value or pleasure associated with it. Or perhaps because you know that no one is going to help you, so it does not seem feasible or worthwhile to give any more time to it than absolutely necessary.

Nurturance and caregiving are notoriously inefficient. Insofar as housekeeping participates in and forms part of the infrastructure for nurturance and care, it makes good sense for housekeeping to be designed not for maximum efficiency but for appropriate redundancy. We need to plan to take enough time to do the work—perhaps not always as much time as might be ideal but enough time that on a normal day most of the things that need to be done can get done and on a hard day there are corners that can be cut.

This might mean taking time to stock the pantry so that the cupboard contains the makings for what cookbooks used to call "emergency dishes"—things you can make by opening a few cans without having to go to the grocery store or picking up the phone for takeout. It might mean taking time to teach the children to fold the laundry or run the vacuum, even though doing it yourself might be faster. Now when you are the one who gets sick, the children are already active participants in the work of the household and are already accustomed to helping to care for you and for one another.

Housekeeping emergencies, whether large or small, are also occasions for the giving and receiving of help. While the rule of modern culture seems often to be that everyone has to manage all alone, all of the time, the impetus of the gospel is in the other direction, toward mutuality and helping one another. Help with the housework is about as basic as such mutuality gets, which is why when somebody dies or somebody is born, the first thing that happens is that people start bringing food over.

It is not always easy either to receive or to give such help, particularly if the occasion is something other than a birth or a death or if the help that is needed goes beyond a casserole or two. It requires a certain vulnerability to admit we need help, a certain humility to accept it, and a life already structured to include time for nurturance if we are to be able to offer it. And yet there are depths of relationship that can be explored only if we are willing to admit our needs to one another and to give and receive help when the opportunity arises.

It is much easier to give and receive help in the midst of large or small household emergencies if we have practiced doing so in nonemergency situations. Sharing marketing or cooking tasks, handing down clothing from one family to another, sharing child care so that each household has a few quiet hours in which to clean—all these are practices that can allow us to form habits of mutual assistance that will inevitably deepen our community lives and that can weave the kinds of bonds between us that will mean we can rely on one another in times of particular need.

WELCOMING AND SENDING

In the classic board game Sorry! the objective of the game is to get all of your playing pieces from the circle marked "Start" to another circle marked "Home." "Home" is insulated from the perimeter of the board by a "safety zone" that no one else's playing pieces may enter, and once a playing piece has reached "Home," it does not leave.

There is a strong tendency in much of modern culture to think of home in terms rather like these. Home is to be a place of safety, of isolation from the cold, hard world out there. People from outside are allowed in only in the most infrequent and controlled circumstances, and although we may have to leave from time to time to go to work or school, home remains as a haven to which we can retreat, whose doors we can close against whomever and whatever we wish to keep out.

How different from this is the picture of home that we find in scripture. For the people of Israel, home is, to be sure, a place of shelter and of protection, but it is not a static fortress. Home is dynamic and movable; its boundaries are permeable, like a tent whose flaps can be extended to make room for more. The prophet Isaiah, envisioning the future of the people of God, says, "Enlarge the place of your tent, and let the curtains of your habitations be stretched out . . . for you will spread abroad to the right and to the left, and your descendants will possess the nations and will people the desolate cities" (Isaiah 54:2, 3).

A godly home is to be a place of nurturance and refreshment not only for its inhabitants but also for strangers and guests. Household members come home not to escape the world and its other inhabitants but to eat and to rest, to enjoy fellowship with one another, and to go back out into the world of work and other people. And a home is to be a place where those who are members of other households— or of none—are regularly welcomed, where the fellowship of the household is enriched and enlarged by the presence of guests. As a Polish proverb puts it, "A guest in the home is God in the home."

Humble, simple surroundings often prove more conducive to hospitality than grander settings. Television commentator Carol Zaleski once identified the TV "home" of Fred Rogers (who was a Presbyterian minister as well as the host of a children's program) as an example in this regard. "Sacred hospitality requires hominess. Therefore Mister Rogers' living room could not keep pace with the current standards for an American home. Where is the open floor plan? Where are the yawning abysses from conversation pit to cathedral ceiling? Instead, we are in a slightly frayed but cozy little sitting room, where we can be ourselves."

"Slightly frayed" is a phrase that could describe the homes of many people I know (not to mention my own). It is an encouragement to remember that a little fraying may be all to the good where hospitality is concerned. We are all of us a little frayed, and that is why we need hospitality, whether we are guests or hosts. God has welcomed us into his household, despite—in fact, because of—our weaknesses and needs, and he invites us even in our not-yet-perfected condition to extend that same welcome to others, promising that as we do so, we will welcome God himself.

Offering welcome in the modern world may look rather different than it looked in ancient times. A young man of my acquaintance was very much struck by the biblical injunction to welcome the stranger and resolved together with his wife that they would invite into their home any stranger

who came to their door. The experiment ended after a few
weeks, during which time, my friend reported ruefully, the
only stranger who knocked on the door was the parcel delivery man, who declined their invitation to come in.

If we want the boundaries of our homes to be flexible
and permeable, we may discover, as my young friend did, that
it is not enough to wait for people to show up of their own
accord. We may need to start issuing invitations. Perhaps there
are people from church or from the neighborhood whom we
would like to know better and who could come for Sunday
lunch or a weekday supper. It is possible that like the king in
Jesus' parable who had trouble finding people to come to his
banquet, we may find our invitations rebuffed by people who
are busy with other things. But it is also possible that if we are
persistent we may, like that king, eventually find people who
are glad to take their places around our table.

Another way to create a welcoming home is to make
the house accessible to a person with a disability. Modern
medicine, far from eliminating disability, has instead extended
the lives of countless people with temporary or permanent
disabilities. Too often, though, inaccessible housing excludes
the disabled from the homes of others or confines them in
their own homes. Those of us who are presently able to climb
stairs with ease often fail to realize that we are likely to find
that seemingly simple action difficult or impossible at some
point in our lives. As one woman said after breaking her ankle
and spending three months in a nonwalking cast, "The house
became a prison."

The typical modern house, with stairs to every exterior
doorway, is indeed a prison to any disabled member of the
household and a fortress to any disabled person outside it. To
these persons, nothing says "welcome" so unmistakably as a
house with a level entrance or a ramp. We may think we have

no need to ramp our homes because we have never had a guest with a disability. It could be, though, that part of the reason we have no such guests is precisely because the house is inaccessible. What was true for baseball in Iowa is true of handicapped access: build it, and they will come.

We can also offer welcome by sharing the amenities of our homes with friends or guests. When my son was small, I had a sitter who came one afternoon a week. She was a college student who lived in a dormitory, so I invited her to bring her laundry with her and to use our washing machine and dryer. She showed up every week with a laundry bag over her shoulder and a smile on her face, as reliable and happy a babysitter as I had ever had. Sharing the laundry facilities had, in fact, the effect of making her more than a babysitter; she became a kind of peripheral member of the household, one who both contributed to the work of the household and benefited from it.

A more all-encompassing form of hospitality is the practice of sharing the household itself, by inviting others to become members of it for a shorter or a longer time. This is not a simple matter, either practically or personally. Making a bedroom for a guest may mean converting a family room or den for that purpose or doubling up children in existing bedrooms. And every time you add a member to a household, you add an extra layer of complexity to relationships within the household. But the mutual giving and receiving that can take place in such shared households can be profound.

The tide of housekeeping can also run from our own homes to those of others as we assist in the provision of food or clothing or shelter to people who are outside our homes. Every congregation and neighborhood includes individuals or families who could use some extra help—meals carried in, clothes for the children, some assistance with housecleaning or seasonal chores. As we begin to make time in our daily routines to do these tasks in our own homes, we may gradually find time to assist others as well, in whatever ways our situations in life allow, so that all may enjoy the comforts and blessings of home.

MEMORY AND HOPE

I have a friend who grew up in a household that was fraught with various tensions. The time when those tensions seemed most noticeably to subside was on the family's annual vacations at a summer cottage owned by her grandparents. Years later, in the midst of mostly happy experiences as a wife and mother, my friend was painting the interior of her house. The job was nearly done when she realized that the colors she had chosen were the colors of her grandparents' summer cottage.

So many of our efforts to make a home are an effort to recover memories of home. Whether it is a parents' or grandparents' home or perhaps the home of another relative or of a friend, many of us have happy memories of home that stay with us throughout our lives and that we long to re-create in our present homes. We treasure inherited objects (a chair, a pair of candlesticks) and practices (a traditional holiday menu, the "right" way to fold a sheet) at least in part because they remind us of home.

These memories of home go deeper than our particular experiences of home. They are part of the communal memory of the church and indeed of the human race itself. There is some level on which we all, individually and together, remember Paradise. We remember a time when God was in his heaven and all really was right with the world, and we wish it were that way still. Even a common reminder to be realistic about the fleetingness of what we remember—"You can't go home again"—discloses an undercurrent of longing for a remembered home.

The good news of the gospel is that the longing for home need not be merely nostalgic. Home is not just a real or imagined memory. Home is also a promise made by God to his people. Indeed, some of Jesus' best-loved descriptions of the kingdom of God are framed explicitly in terms of home: "In my Father's house are many rooms," he tells his disciples as they gather around a supper table on the night before he died. "If it were not so, would I have told you that I go to prepare a place for you? And when I go and prepare a place for you, I will come again and will take you to myself, that where I am you may be also" (John 14:2, 3).

As much as this is a promise for the future, it is not only for the future. "If a man loves me," Jesus says, "he will keep my word, and my Father will love him, and we will come to him and make our home with him" (John 14:23). This is a promise that involves the body as well as the soul. The Christian community is not a spiritual club; it is a household, God's own household (Ephesians 2:19), whose very sacraments are physical acts evocative of home: a bath and a meal.

A well-kept house thus possesses a kind of sacramental quality. It is no substitute for either the kingdom of God or the church. But it is a kind of foretaste of the kingdom. A nurturing and hospitable home can be a reminder that God has always been in the business of making a home for people, that God desires that people should have the food and clothing and shelter associated with home, that one day our tattered and partial provision of these things for one another will be gloriously supplanted by God's perfect provision of shining robes and a sumptuous feast in God's own house.

This sacramental quality of home means that a well-kept house is a means to an end, not an end in itself. Faithfully keeping house is a way to remember God's promises of home and actively to anticipate the fulfillment of those promises. It participates in these promises by ministering to humans' basic needs for food and clothing and shelter, and it points beyond these temporal and partial satisfactions to the One who is himself preparing a room and a meal and a garment for each of us.

Our aim in keeping house cannot therefore be to do so "perfectly," because that is someone else's job (namely, God's). Our aim is much more modest: to practice "good enough" housekeeping. None of us needs a perfectly kept home. Indeed, we are likely to find homes that seem to be perfectly kept rather off-putting. But we all need homes in which the housekeeping is good enough, in which basic needs are provided for rather than neglected and in which welcome and care are routinely and cheerfully extended to both members and guests of the household.

Good enough housekeeping can take many different forms. Just as there are many ways to nurture a child, there are many ways to keep house. Cultural norms vary widely, as do personal preferences. And the seasons of our lives and of our houses change as well. The lively disorder of a household with young children gives way in time to the tranquillity of an empty nest, which itself may undergo change as adults retire or their careers evolve and their relationships to the house and housekeeping evolve as well.

Throughout our lives, housekeeping can play a part in the ancient Christian discipline of the imitation of Christ. In his earthly life, Jesus humbly embraced both life in the body and life in community. He allowed others to feed and shelter him and in turn concerned himself with the feeding and clothing and sheltering of others. And he encouraged his followers to feed the hungry, give drink to the thirsty, clothe the naked, and welcome the stranger, saying that in so doing, they were doing these things for him.

As we thus obey and imitate Christ in caring for people in these basic ways, we remember him and his ministry and presence among humans, and we anticipate the day when we will see him face to face in God the Father's house. Remembering both Jesus and Eden itself, longing for Paradise, living faithfully with one another between the times—these are the things that people do at home. As we participate with one another in the litany of daily life, we foster these memories and these hopes.

And as we do so, we join all God's people in the ancient song sung by the psalmist: "How lovely is thy dwelling place, O Lord of Hosts! My soul longs, yea, faints for the courts of the Lord; my heart and flesh sing for joy to the living God. Even the sparrow finds a home, and the swallow a nest for herself, where she may lay her young, at thy altars, O Lord of Hosts, my King and my God. Blessed are those who dwell in thy house, ever singing thy praise!" (Psalm 84:1–4).

CHAPTER ONE
WHAT'S CHRISTIAN ABOUT HOUSEWORK?

Designer cleaning products: Ruth La Ferla, "On the Shelf of a Goddess, Gathering Dust," *New York Times*, April 7, 2002, sec. 9, p. 1.

Models posing on washing machines: Robert Trachtenberg and Elizabeth Stewart, "The Spin Cycle, *New York Times Magazine*, September 21, 2003, pp. 66–67.

Home as a total haven: "Stacey," quoted in Judy Dutton, "Meet the New Housewife Wanna-bes," *Cosmopolitan*, June 2000, p. 164.

"Domesticity" magazine ad: *Martha Stewart Living*, April 2002.

Statistics on housework: Dirk Johnson, "Until Dust Do Us Part," *Newsweek*, March 25, 2002, p. 41.

Meals prepared or eaten away from home: Jean Zimmerman, *Made from Scratch: Reclaiming the Pleasures of the American Hearth* (New York: Free Press, 2003), p. 153.

No responsibility for housework: Arlie Russell Hochschild, *The Time Bind: When Work Becomes Home and Home Becomes Work* (New York: Holt, 1997).

Who is doing housework: Cathi Hanauer (ed.), *The Bitch in the House: 26 Women Tell the Truth About Sex, Solitude, Work, Motherhood, and Marriage* (New York: Morrow, 2002); Daniel Jones (ed.), *The Bastard on the Couch: 27 Men Try Really Hard to*

Explain Their Feelings About Love, Loss, Fatherhood, and Freedom
(New York: Morrow, 2002).

Origins of housework: Ruth Schwartz Cowan, *More Work for
Mother: The Ironies of Household Technology from the Open Hearth
to the Microwave* (New York: Basic Books, 1983), p. 18.

Germaine Greer: Quoted in Lesley Johnson and Justine Lloyd,
"Domestic Bliss!" *New Humanist,* November 1, 2004, http://
www.newhumanist.org.uk/volume119issue6_more.php?id=10
59_0_33_0_C.

Incompetence of housewives: Joan Williams, "How Academe
Treats Mothers," *Chronicle of Higher Education,* June 17, 2002,
http://chronicle.com/jobs/2002/06/2002061701c.htm.

Housekeeping manuals: Karen Kingston, *Clear Your Clutter with
Feng Shui* (New York: Broadway Books, 1998); Gary Thorp,
Sweeping Changes: Discovering the Joy of Zen in Everyday Tasks
(New York: Broadway Books, 2000); Marla Cilley, *Sink
Reflections* (New York: Bantam Books, 2002).

Overscheduled readers: Robin Domeniconi, quoted in David
Carr, "Don't Aspire; Just Embrace Simplicity, Magazines Say,"
New York Times, December 9, 2002, p. C11.

The torture of housework: Simone de Beauvoir, quoted in
Marianne Rohrlich, "Swabbing the Deck: Mop Tops and
Top Mops," *New York Times,* April 18, 2002, p. F1.

Repetition: Søren Kierkegaard, quoted in Kathleen Norris,
The Quotidian Mysteries: Laundry, Liturgy, and "Women's Work"
(Mahwah, N.J.: Paulist Press, 1998), p. 28.

CHAPTER TWO
A PLACE TO LIVE

Hugh of Saint Cher: Quoted in Stanley Hauerwas and Will
Willimon, *Where Resident Aliens Live: Exercises for Christian
Practice* (Nashville, Tenn.: Abingdon Press, 1996), p. 24.

Malcolm Muggeridge: Quoted in ibid., p. 25.

Lighting the kitchen with appliance bulbs: Julienne Bennett and
Mimi Luebbermann, *Where the Heart Is: A Celebration of Home*

(Berkeley, Calif.: Wildcat Canyon Press and New World Library, 1995).

Images of home: Drawn in part from Marjorie O'Rourke Boyle, *Divine Domesticity: Augustine of Thagaste to Teresa of Avila* (Leiden, Netherlands: Brill, 1997), pp. ix–x.

More single-person households: Sam Roberts, "Married Becomes a Minority Status," *Philadelphia Inquirer*, October 15, 2006, p. A17.

Wanting a wife: Judy Syfers [Brady], "I Want a Wife," *Ms.*, Spring 1972, p. 56.

"Housework" quote: Sheldon Harnick, "Housework," *Ms.*, November 1972 (Volume 1, Issue 5), p. 96.

Men don't care about housework: Kathy Fitzgerald Sherman, *A Housekeeper Is Cheaper Than a Divorce: Why You Can Afford to Hire Help and How to Get It* (Mountain View, Calif.: Life Tools Press, 2000).

Doing only important things: Lisa Earle McLeod, quoted in *Real Simple*, April 2002.

Janitorial and creative housewifery: Barbara Holland, *In Private Life* (Pleasantville, N.Y.: Akadine Press, 2000), p. 199.

CHAPTER THREE
SHELTERING A HOUSEHOLD

Reciprocal relationship between buildings and their contexts: See the "Cities and Towns" issue of *Christian Reflection,* published by the Center for Christian Ethics at Baylor University.

House size: Sarah Susanka, *The Not-So-Big House* (Newtown, Conn.: Taunton, 1998).

Binge and purge: Niecy Nash, "The Lady of the House Talks Hair Collections, Dirty Clothes and Obeying the Urge to Purge," 2006, http://www.stylenetwork.com/Shows/CleanHouse/Meet/index.html.

Reusing food cans: "Why Not Simplify Your Life This Month?" *Real Simple*, April 2004, p. 14.

Reusing orange rinds: Melissa Page and Ashley Tate, "Solutions: New Uses for Old Things," *Real Simple,* August 2006, p. 48.

Samuel Pepys' bookpresses: Henry Petroski, *The Book on the Bookshelf* (New York: Knopf, 1999), p. 126.

Common cup versus individual cups for communion: Daniel Sack, *Whitebread Protestants: Food and Religion in American Culture* (New York: St. Martin's Press, 2000), pp. 12–58.

CHAPTER FOUR
CLOTHES TO WEAR

Little Bear: Else Holmelund Minarik, *Little Bear,* illus. Maurice Sendak (New York: HarperCollins, 1957).

Wealthy women who buy designer clothing in black: Ellyn Spragins, "This Old Thing? I've Had It Forever," *New York Times,* April 15, 2001, sec. 3, p. 13.

Choosing jeans: Barry Schwartz, *The Paradox of Choice: Why More Is Less* (New York: Ecco, 2004), pp. 1–2.

"You can't fit me": Ginia Bellafante, "Stepping Out in Stepford Style," *New York Times,* October 20, 2002, sec. 9, p. 8.

The Princess package: Jodi Kantor, "Love the Riches, Lose the Rags," *New York Times,* November 2, 2005, p. G1.

Formal dinner parties: Robert Farrar Capon, *The Supper of the Lamb: A Culinary Reflection* (New York: Farrar, Straus & Giroux, 1967), p. 178.

Legacy to one's daughter: Ruth La Ferla, "Like It? I Did It Myself, Darling," *New York Times,* Oct. 14, 2001, sec. 9, p. 1.

What any knitter knows: Elaine Eskesen, "Found Pattern," in *KnitLit,* ed. Linda Roghaar and Molly Wolf (New York: Three Rivers Press, 2002), p. 67.

Refinishing chairs during pastoral calls: Edith Schaeffer, *The Hidden Art of Homemaking* (Wheaton, Ill.: Tyndale House, 1971), p. 71.

The need to make something: Connie Elizabeth Tintinalli, "You Have to Make Something," in *KnitLit,* p. 138.

CHAPTER FIVE
CLOTHING A HOUSEHOLD

Doing laundry better than anyone else: Lisa Wlodarski Romano, quoted in Emily Harrison Weir, "Bragging Rights: Unusual and Often Unsung Alumnae Talents," *Mount Holyoke Alumnae Quarterly*, Spring 2006, p. 24.

Folding sheets: Julianne Trabucci Puckett, quoted in ibid., p. 25.

Shopping as a party: Amanda Kovattana, "Closet Space," March 7, 2006, http://amandakovattana.blogspot.com/2006/03/closet-space.html.

Lenten inventory: Joan Chittister, *Wisdom Distilled from the Daily: Living the Rule of St. Benedict Today* (San Francisco: HarperSanFrancisco, 1990), p. 73.

Laundry lust: Pilar Viladas, "Laundry Lust," *New York Times Magazine*, September 21, 2003, p. 65.

Washing machine advertisement: Ad for the Bosch "Nexxt" washer and dryer, *Real Simple*, June 2003.

Never mending: Holland, *In Private Life*, pp. 104–105.

The tension between mending and throwing things out: Comments posted at http://www.berkeley.parents.edu.

Extreme ironing: Pam Belluck, "Get Out Your Boards: Extreme Ironing May Soon Be Hot," *New York Times*, May 21, 2004, p. A14.

Martha-prayer: Molly Wolf, "Dance, Then . . . ," in *Hiding in Plain Sight: Sabbath Blessings* (Collegeville, Minn.: Liturgical Press, 1998), pp. 109–112.

The closet as paean to our possessions: Kovattana, "Closet Space."

Bungalow closets: Ann Patchett, "Invasion of the PODS," *Preservation*, March-April 2006, pp. 18–19.

CHAPTER SIX
FOOD TO EAT

Capon on calories: Robert Farrar Capon, *The Supper of the Lamb*, p. 112.

Every meal anticipating the heavenly banquet: Stephen H. Webb, in his review of Marion Nestle's *Food Politics* in *The Christian Century,* April 10–17, 2002, p. 36. See also his *Good Eating* (Grand Rapids, Mich.: Brazos Press, 2001), which advocates Christian vegetarianism.

John Woolman story: Mark A. Noll, *A History of Christianity in the United States and Canada* (Grand Rapids, Mich.: Eerdmans, 1992), p. 68.

Supermarket as vending machine: Gary Paul Nabham, *Coming Home to Eat: The Pleasures and Politics of Local Foods* (New York: Norton, 2002), p. 13.

Not having to cook anymore: Amanda Hesser, "Basic Instinct," *New York Times Magazine,* April 14, 2002, p. 63.

Not cooking to spend time with grandchildren: Melanie Warner, "New Frontiers in Takeout: Family-Style Restaurants Deliver Food to Cars at Curbside, for Meals That Nobody at Home Had to Cook," *New York Times,* June 6, 2006, p. C1.

Food photography: Patricia Leigh Brown, "Living Large: Getting the Cheesecake Shot, *New York Times,* October 13, 2002, sec. 4, p. 6.

CHAPTER SEVEN
FEEDING A HOUSEHOLD

Everyday cooking: Capon, *Supper of the Lamb,* p. 23.

Feeding children: Ibid., p. 131.

Using prepackaged ingredients: Sandra Lee, quoted in Amanda Hesser, "Homemade or Semi? A Bake-Off," *New York Times,* October 1, 2003, p. F1.

Beefy taco joes: Advertisement for Campbell's soup, *Martha Stewart Living,* April 2002.

Cleaning up after Mass: Norris, *Quotidian Mysteries,* p. 2.

CHAPTER EIGHT
THE WELL-KEPT HOUSE

Hospitality as a moral pillar of society: For a discussion of this, see Christine Pohl, *Making Room: Recovering Hospitality as a Christian Tradition* (Grand Rapids, Mich.: Eerdmans, 1999), esp. pp. 3–15.

Polish proverb: Quoted in Evelyn Vitz, *A Continual Feast: A Cookbook to Celebrate the Joys of Family and Faith Throughout the Christian Year* (New York: HarperCollins, 1985), p. 68.

Mr. Rogers's living room: Carol Zaleski, "Mister Rogers," *The Christian Century,* April 19, 2003, p. 35.

Woman with broken ankle: Quoted in Larry Armstrong, "Remodeling for the Future," *Business Week,* July 25, 2005, p. 104.

THE AUTHOR

Margaret Kim Peterson is theologian in residence at First Presbyterian Church, Norristown, Pennsylvania. She grew up in Mount Vernon, Iowa, and though now a long-time resident of the East Coast, she returns to the Midwest whenever possible. A graduate of Mount Holyoke College, Gordon-Conwell Theological Seminary, and Duke University, she now teaches theology at Eastern University in St. Davids, Pennsylvania. She is married to Dwight N. Peterson, who also teaches at Eastern University. Together they are the parents of a son, Mark.